P9-AOR-913

Corporate Instinct

Corporate Instinct

Building a Knowing Enterprise for the 21st Century

Thomas Koulopoulos
Richard Spinello
Wayne Toms

Van Nostrand Reinhold
I T P® A Division of International Thomson Publishing Inc.

New York • Albany • Bonn • Boston • Detroit • London • Madrid • Melbourne
Mexico City • Paris • San Francisco • Singapore • Tokyo • Toronto

The ideas presented in this book are generic and strategic. Their specific application to a
particular company must be the responsibility of the management of that company, based
on management's understanding of their company's procedures, culture, resources, and
competitive situation.

Printed in the United States of America

http://www.vnr.com   Visit us on the Web!

For more information contact:

Van Nostrand Reinhold
115 Fifth Avenue
New York, NY 10003
USA

Chapman & Hall GmbH
Pappalallee 3
69469 Weinham
Germany

Chapman & Hall
2-6 Boundary Row
London SEI 8HN
United Kingdom

International Thomson Publishing Asia
60 Albert Street #15-01
Albert Complex
Singapore 189969

Thomas Nelson Australia
102 Dodds Street
South Melbourne 3205
Victoria, Australia

International Thomson Publishing Japan
Hirakawa-cho Kyowa Building, 3F
2-2-1 Hirakawa-cho, Chiyoda-ku
Tokyo 102 Japan

Nelson Canada
1120 Birchmount Road
Scarborough, Ontario
M1K 5G4, Canada

International Thomson Editores
Seneca, 53
Colonia Polanco
11560 Mexico D.F. Mexico

1 2 3 4 5 6 7 8 9 10 QEBFF 01 00 99 98 97

Library of Congress Cataloging-in-Publication Data

Koulopoulos, Thomas M.
    Corporate instinct : building a knowing enterprise for the 21st
century / Thomas Koulopoulos, Richard Spinello, Wayne Toms.
       p.   cm.
    Includes bibliographical references and index.
    ISBN 0-442-02622-6
    1. Organizational learning. 2. Corporate culture. I. Spinello,
Richard A.   II. Toms, Wayne.   III. Title.
HD58.82.K68   1997
658.4' 06--dc21   97-36696

HD
58.82
K68
1997

Production: Jo-Ann Campbell • mle design • 213 Cider Mill Road, Glastonbury, CT 06033

To my grandparents,
Tasso & Marika, Nicholas & Angeliki—
whose love gave me the confidence to follow my
instincts

T.K.

To Susan—
for her wise counsel and loving support

R.S.

To my parents—
who taught me how to think

W.T.

CONTENTS

Acknowledgments

The idea that became the seed for *Corporate Instinct* was planted more than two years ago. Since then it has had the benefit of countless contributors, supporters, and critics. As authors, it was our responsibility to articulate the idea, but its evolution rests firmly on the bedrock of support that we received from many individuals. Foremost among these are our clients and the companies discussed in the book. Both have played a valuable role in formulating the precepts of corporate instinct through their fundamental belief in the unlimited power of human innovation. We are especially grateful to the hundreds of individuals who participated in the early Corporate IQ test. Their insights and attitudes have been critical in formulating our own views on corporate instinct and in demonstrating its value to successful organizations.

Among those who helped us to create the book, none had greater perseverance than our agent, John Willig, who nurtured the original manuscript through three proposals over a period of nearly a year. John's soft-spoken manner was critical when it needed to be, but his commitment to the project was unwavering. John Boyd, our Publisher at Van Nostrand Reinhold, saw the early potential in the book and helped to provide the initial structure for organizing the many concepts included. John and our Senior Editor, Tony Vlamis, also lead the Van Nostrand Reinhold team which, from the initial meeting complete with chicken soup for one of the ailing authors, made it clear that this was the sort of organization where the idea of corporate instinct would be right at home. Our developmental editor, Jayne Pearl, worked around the clock, with at least one known nap at the keyboard, while trying to restructure the original manuscript under incredibly tight deadlines. She questioned everything and we got away with nothing. Any confusion that remains in the book is probably attributable to our not taking her advice. The production team, including Jo-Ann Campbell, at mle design, Chris Bates and Carl German at VNR, worked their usual magic by putting the manuscript through its final paces.

Then there are the thought leaders whose input helped us form our ideas and validate our assumptions. Many graciously contributed time to read the manuscript and provide comments on its many iterations. Among those we would like to single out are: Geoffrey James, one of the first people to see the proposal for *Corporate Instinct,* who was quick to offer support and advice on the nuances of publishing such an aggressive project; Jonathan Foster-Pedley, Professor at the University of Cape Town, who provided feedback on the article which eventually turned into this book; Jeffrey Miller of Documentum, Jay Tanna of Altris, and Larry Bohn, former president of PC DOCS, who were all sounding boards for the initial *BusinessWeek* section on corporate instinct; Bob Guns for his thorough review of the book and insights into knowledge management; Paul Strassmann for his honest and tenured critique; and Jim Champy, who has provided encouragement and wisdom as a generous mentor and muse.

We would be remiss to leave out the valuable insights of the Delphi team—an amazing group of talented, energetic, and innovative individuals who form the very essence of corporate instinct. We offer our special thanks to the core team, Carl, Debra, Nick, MaryAnn, Nat, Carlene, Linda,

Dan, Aleise, John, Kristine, Andrea, Michael, Rich, Hadley, and Kristi—whose individual and collective efforts prove daily that innovation has no bounds.

Finally, it is the enduring support and, at times, outright tolerance of our friends and families that made the task of writing *Corporate Instinct* worthwhile—indeed even possible. The list includes simple gestures and profound sacrifices. All are important, including: Rona's vote of confidence—enclosed in a late night e-mail; Debbie's proofing in between bouts of chasing an overactive, yet adorable, two year-old; Keith's refresher course on the aerodynamics of wind sheer (you'll have to read the book) and his wife Judy's forbearance putting up with yet another seaside vacation listening to the waves breaking over the incessant tapping of a laptop's keyboard; and so many more that we simply cannot list here.

As authors, we are able to recoup something tangible for all of the trials which writing entails. It is small recompense, however, when measured against the greater reward of knowing these very special people. We hope the results are worthy of their support.

Introduction

I live in a 200-year-old house that is still heated by 100-year-old steam radiators. Despite the advantages of the last hundred years in heating systems, steam is still one of the most efficient and comfortable ways to heat a house. Except for one slight problem. The exposed radiators can be scalding to an unaware visitor.

Two years after buying our old home our first daughter, Mia came along. I was panic-stricken as Mia grew beyond the toddler stage and began exploring the house. But she never once scalded herself. She quickly developed a keen sense of when the radiator was on and always kept a safe distance.

As a child, I melted all sorts of objects—crayons, toy soldiers, my mother's "nylons"—as experiments to test how these various items, and my parents, would hold up. Of course, Mia would test the *concept* of heat by running her hand close to a radiator, pointing to it on occasion and telling us it was *hot*. But never once did she need to touch it to tell it was hot. Like many new parents, I had severely underestimated her ability to understand and adapt to the world around her.

I have no illusion. Mia will eventually burn herself, as most children do, if not on the radiator then somehow, somewhere. But the wonder of the human mind is that it is wired to make connections between accepted truths, pieces of otherwise unlinked information, thereby connecting concept and reality in such a way that even a toddler can *know* what it means to be *hot,* without needing to fully experience scalding heat. These links create an ability akin to a sixth sense that helps us to navigate successfully through the world by giving us the capacity to visualize the future results of our actions.

What does Mia have to do with organizations and the topic of corporate instinct? Ask yourself this question: How close does your organization have to get to the fire to know it is hot?

If you're still struggling with the answer, let's make it a bit more real. Imagine yourself seated at a fancy Japanese steak house—the kind where eight to twelve people are crowded around a sizzling stove-top table. Now hold your hand out in front of you about six inches above the hot table top. Close your eyes and imagine how the dissipating heat would feel at six inches.

Now consider yourself as a metaphor for your company. Your hand is the company's ability to sense a new market, or a shift in the market. And the heat is the intensity of that market shift. Slowly begin lowering your hand and stop when the heat is intense enough for the company to take positive action.

How close did you get? Five inches? Two? Barely touching the surface? Some companies need to smell burning flesh before they take action. Even then, the action may be to figure out what the smell is—not remove the hand! The motto these companies seem to follow is, "Where there's smoke, there's a committee."

How many markets pass companies by, how many new opportunities get grabbed up by competitors, how many employees take good ideas elsewhere because their companies lack an awareness of themselves, their abilities, and their markets? In short, how many companies fail to feel the heat of the market before it's too late?

Why is it that some companies react while others are rendered helplessly numb?

Microsoft came to market with an inferior user interface in the 1980s and early 1990s, trailing behind Apple's extraordinary user interface. Its inferior Internet strategy in the mid-1990s lost ground to that of wunderkind Netscape. New models for computing, such as Oracle's NC (Networked Computer), are the latest challenge to Microsoft's edge. Yet, Microsoft has continued and is likely to continue coming out on top. How? Microsoft simply keeps putting out products. It keeps reevaluating even its most popular and profitable products and strategies and constantly comes out with new and improved versions. The process, some would say, drives its customers crazy—more to the point, it drives its competition insane!

So while Apple has been fearful about making profound changes in its products, Microsoft eagerly improved Windows 3.1 with its rollout of Windows 95. Industry experts believed Microsoft was slitting its own throat, that no one would upgrade. Clearly, the pundits were wrong. Microsoft knows its strength is in desktop computers. What desktop computers will look like is secondary to the company maintaining its leading edge. To do so, Microsoft has no reluctance to cannibalize its own products.

Compare these instincts with those of the 1980s Digital Equipment Corporation. DEC responded to the threat of personal computers by attempting to compete with IBM in the ebbing mainframe computer market and introducing a new generation of mainframes.

Which one was better able to feel the heat, DEC or Microsoft? Both had extraordinary resources, in people and finances. In fact, during its 1987 DECWORLD conference in Boston, Digital Equipment actually leased the QEII for a week simply to hold evening parties for prospects, partners, and clients. There was no lack of financial or creative resources at DEC.

I recall a conversation on the deck of the QEII with a DEC employee who speculated whether Ken Olsen, founder and then president of DEC, would pursue the PC market. At the time it was a matter of great debate at DEC, although middle management and just about every salesperson at DEC could have answered the question as easily as my two-year-old daughter can tell when the radiator is hot by the whistling steam valve and banging pipes.

There are countless examples of companies that were nearly engulfed in flames, yet still lacked the ability to sense the heat and react to the market. It is far too easy to chalk this ineptitude up to simplistic market positioning, poor management skills, or inadequate financial resources. Especially when the most notable failures have involved companies whose health and prosperity were unquestionable when they fell from grace.

What then is the problem? How can companies feel the heat before it's too late to take action, before their competency fades into complacency? To probe these questions, we interviewed 350 organizations. The most successful of these companies shared similar attitudes, organizational structures, and, most important, a knack for ignoring their own corporate memory when good ideas came along. Their answers, sprinkled throughout the book, along with anecdotes and case studies of companies on various points along the spectrum of responsiveness lead to the formulation of three key concepts: *corporate instinct,* which is the sixth sense the companies exhibited; the *knowledge chain,* which was the mechanism of their success; and the *knowing enterprise,* which is how we characterize these highly responsive and aware companies.

The most important and consistent trait in these companies was an ability to unlearn as quickly as they re-learned, thereby pushing aside their own best ideas for new ones that meet the rapidly changing markets they inhabit.

Arie de Geus, in his book *The Living Company*, describes many such companies that have survived far beyond the average corporate life cycle of twenty years—companies such as Stora, a Swedish chemical manufacturer that started off as a copper mine 700 years ago.

De Geus and his researchers at Royal Dutch Shell found that "across the Northern Hemisphere, average corporate life expectancy was well below twenty years. Only the large companies [they] studied, which had started to expand after they survived infancy (during which the mortality rate is extremely high) continued to live, on average, another twenty to thirty years."

In fact, more than half of all the companies in the Fortune's Top 100 industrial group ten years ago are no longer there, and long protected industries have been completely restructured.

Companies like Stora have surely been innovative, but after the turmoil of the 1980s and 1990s, every astute manager recognizes the need for constant innovation and the ability to react rapidly to change. Recognizing the need for agility and reengineering is only a diagnosis; it is not a prescription for change. What was still missing was a concrete set of tools and *a unifying framework* that would enable organizations to react and reform on a continuous basis.

Corporate instinct is such a framework. It is also a new way of thinking about organizations and a novel way of applying specific technology tools (most of which you already have).

Your organization most likely has an information technology system infrastructure, such as a database and e-mail. You may even be starting to think of a knowledge management system to manage digital information that employees constantly create. That information represents your organization's competitive edge.

How are you using that digital information? Are you burying it by putting it into systems that don't allow you to reevaluate the context in which the knowledge was originally created? Are you focusing all of your energy on getting knowledge out of your information systems or are you considering how to get it in, perhaps even how to turn that energy into knowledge? The promise of corporate instinct —the ability to sense the market, access your organization's resources and competencies, and act instantaneously—can only be realized if you capture and organize internally and externally generated knowledge in a way that creates an intimacy and awareness in the organization of why things are being done the way they're being done.

All of this sounds relatively straightforward until it comes time to put it into practice. Although the concept of corporate instinct may be easy to grasp, it requires changing attitudes and some very strongly held beliefs. It also requires constant vigilance—what Andy Grove, Intel's Chairman, describes as a fair measure of "paranoia." This book is a detailed road map intended to provide you with a case for developing your own corporate instinct and a comprehensive context for understanding how and why corporate instinct offers enduring competitive advantage.

The book is divided into four parts that will guide you through corporate instinct: the basic principles of corporate instinct, how to apply and manage it, the economic and social imperative to create instinct, and finally a Corporate IQ test for evaluating your own corporate instinct quotient.

A quick tour of the book will help you better understand its structure and the variety of new concepts presented.

- Part I begins by differentiating between instinct as it is commonly defined when referring to the animal kingdom, and how it is defined within the context of an organization. It then distinguishes corporate instinct from *corporate memory,* and describes how a strong corporate memory can become the water wheel that shackles an organization to a single stream of thought, making it difficult to move into new markets and take advantage of new opportunities. The *knowledge chain* will provide a glimpse of how an organization can overcome its corporate memory by focusing on its *internal/external awareness/responsiveness,* allowing it to accelerate the speed of its innovation and more effectively compete. Most important, Part I will review the *eight attitudes* of organizations, which embrace corporate instinct, thereby transforming themselves into a *knowing enterprise*—an organization that is constantly aware of itself, and responsive to its business and market environment.

- Part II delves deeper into the concept of the *knowledge chain* and describes how it is facilitated or impeded by the structure of an organization. Part II also introduces a new means of organizational structure that hinges more on time than on form, the *perpetual organization.* The role of *metaskills* and *communities of practice* will be introduced here, as well as the importance of balancing the chaos of fast innovation with the necessary *coordination* of an organization's resources. Finally, we review some of the specific technologies that can be used to create corporate instinct.

- Part III reviews the economic, managerial, and social context for corporate instinct. It focuses on how radical changes in the very rules of economics and the valuation of organizations, as well as workers, are leading to the inevitability of corporate instinct as a competitive cornerstone. Part III also looks carefully at the leadership styles and qualities that are essential for an instinctive organization to thrive, and the ways that executives can cultivate corporate instinct. Finally, we review the virtues of an instinctive organization and the compelling reasons to adopt this new concept in your organization.

- The appendixes introduce the Corporate IQ test—a brief test to measure your own corporate instinct and to rank it against the hundreds of organizations that have already taken the test.

Any company that has even a modicum of success has instinct. If you are able to react to the market more quickly than your competition, even if only by the grace of dumb luck, you have tapped into your company's instinct. But most corporate success stories are short stories, not epic novels. They are like the many rock bands from the 1960s and 1970s that made the charts with a hit song, never to be heard from again. Doing it once may get you in the limelight, but it won't get you into the Hall of Fame. Corporate instinct is about developing your organization's ability to feel the heat, using its sixth sense of the market, and perpetuating success.

PART ONE

Awakening Corporate Instinct

*Every human mind is a great slumbering power until awakened
by a keen desire and by definite resolution to do.*

Edgar F. Roberts

1

Corporate Instinct and the Knowing Enterprise

We know more than we can tell.

**Michael Polanyi,
Twentieth-century philosopher, Scientist**

OVERCOMING THE PAST

Corporate instinct is a company's collective sixth sense enabling it to overcome its own memory and respond instantaneously and effectively to market opportunity, customers, and competition.

Corporate instinct is simply an innate ability to react in the *right* way, despite the memory of how things have been done. It is an antidote for the chronic syndrome of past success. Corporate instinct allows a company to achieve repeated and extraordinary success without being shackled by its position, memory, and culture.

But the concept of *corporate instinct* seems counterintuitive. Perhaps the only instincts you have observed in an organization are those of lemmings to the cliff, sharks to blood, and wolves on the lone deer. Indeed, we are not accustomed to thinking of companies as having instinct—yet they absolutely do. Don't confuse corporate instinct with animal instinct, which is genetically imprinted, and not likely to be changed through intention. Corporate instinct is the result of deliberate actions. It can be developed. And it is essential.

But just as the concept of corporate culture took some time for people to digest, and is now widely acknowledged, corporate instinct is a new idea that will undoubtedly take time to absorb.

One reason is that corporate instinct is a disturbing idea. We tend to associate instinct strictly with animal instinct, such as that of bees building nests, birds migrating south for the winter—mindless organisms acting in preprogrammed ways. However, when *corporations* act instinctively they are acting beyond the confines of rational control, past memory, or systematic analysis; they are creating strategy from a *collective* reflex.

The premise of corporate instinct is that strategy is not just formulated in full detail in some mountain retreat by a group of strategists who then expect others in the organization to execute that strategy. But it is far from mindless. In fact, in many cases a coherent and intelligible pattern of activities results and a viable strategic direction emerges from what appear to be responses to market forces that are not yet obvious.

In its simplest form, the sixth sense we are referring to when we define corporate instinct is *the collective wisdom that informs decisions and implicitly shapes strategic directions*. An instinctive organization is influenced by the collective wisdom of its employees. But in most organizations, that wisdom is fragmented and scattered throughout the company's culture, systems, structures, procedures, and processes. For a company to tap into and intensify its corporate instinct, everyone must be able to access the organization's collective wisdom. That can only occur when it is infused into the culture, systems, and structures of the organization.

In the course of our interviews with 350 organizations to determine their current state of corporate instinct, an incredible 50 percent claimed that their good ideas were more likely to end up being buried by bureaucracy, ignored, or frustrating employees to go off and start a new company rather than capitalize on the ideas in their current organization! The culprit here is most often the deeply ingrained bureaucracy that stymies any ideas that dare to deviate from tradition and the belief that environmental stability can be controlled from within the organization.

Instinctive organizations let new ideas rush in. They counteract old habits and are set apart from their competitors by adhering zealously to three basic rules.

- They survive based on core competencies, *not* on core products.

- They continuously compete with their own best ideas and make them obsolete.

- They value the acquisition of new knowledge over the creation of corporate structure and standards.

These three rules of corporate instinct are necessary components of *any* enterprise whose mission is to reach beyond the opportunistic success of a first product, or the shortened life cycles of any single product or service in today's fast-paced markets. For example, corporate instinct encourages a company to outgrow a solid market position of the kind that has shackled Xerox to the image of a copier company. Many new and innovative ideas have been spawned from Xerox's Palo Alto Research Center (PARC), including the computer industries' most popular networking standard, ethernet, and the icon-based graphical desktop metaphor that later became the Apple user interface and ultimately the metaphor for all desktop computing. Despite these innovations, Xerox was unable to bring many of its own good ideas to market. To do so, Xerox, and any company that intends to create corporate instinct, must purposefully eclipse the success of yesterday's products and develop new ones before a competitor inevitably does. Most important, it must compete based on its ability to create knowledge constantly—not simply manage the knowledge that it already has.

To Xerox's credit, its recent formation of Xerox New Enterprises, a holding company intended to commercialize ideas from PARC through separate companies, has spawned no less than fifty new products through autonomous organizations. This liberates new ideas from the Xerox corporate memory and allows them to flourish in new companies with their own corporate instinct. This may, in fact, be the only way to capitalize on many of the good ideas spawned by many knowledge-rich companies. In the case of one XNE company, Documentum, a $10 million investment on the part of Xerox has already yielded a $200 million return. These are the sorts of innovations that would never have turned a profit under the traditional organization of Xerox. (This is especially interesting because Documentum has turned only a slight profit since its public offering. In other words, Xerox would have probably not even recouped its initial investment if it had held onto Documentum as a subsidiary.)

This is essential to understand, because the knowledge on which corporate instinct is based is easily mistaken for corporate memory. In a corporate setting, memory is most often associated with informal means of information capture and retrieval, a far less reliable basis for decision making than knowledge. Memory is selective and subjective. Knowledge, or more specifically a knowledgebase, provides specific mechanisms by which to objectify, capture, and make available the collective experiences of an organization.

Corporate memory is not inherently good or bad. It allows employees to collaborate without sophisticated dialogue or explicit, on-going instructions. This can be extremely beneficial, when employees understand the history of that memory and analyze its usefulness in the context of the present environment. Memory and corporate culture—from shared values to written policies and procedures—are part of any organization, however young, however small, or in whatever industry. The ability to anticipate and deliver on a market need, a memory of previous success and failure, and a unifying set of beliefs are all essential ingredients in creating a successful company. Yet these same characteristics can, as we will see, become a company's greatest liability.

A dramatic example of the importance of reevaluating past memory is that of commercial airline pilots' reactions to the threat of microbursts, the severe and often unpredictable downdrafts that occur spontaneously in areas of severe weather turbulence, such as thunderstorms and fast moving weather fronts. A microburst at a lower altitude, especially during a takeoff or landing, can have drastic consequences as it literally slams an airplane back toward the ground. Until recently, pilots relied on an intuitive and standard response to a microburst: add power and pull up—fast! This was in fact a memory response dictated by the knowledge of how airplanes respond to their environment. It was assumed that the faster a pilot took these accepted measures the faster the plane would recover.

It now appears that the organizational memory was wrong—dead wrong in many cases. The current course of action at low altitudes is almost completely counterintu-

itive. When a microburst slams a plane downward, pilots
no longer pull up. Instead, they simply increase speed by
adding power, thereby flying through the microburst,
which is, as the name implies, a fairly short and very confined area of turbulence. When pilots pulled up and added
power, they effectively slowed down the plane, thereby
remaining in the microburst and making it take longer to
recover. By adding power and, more important, flying
through the microburst, pilots reduce the time the plane
has to recover. Neither option is especially pleasant and
the objective is ultimately to detect and avoid the situation, but as in business, turbulence can strike at the most
unexpected times, in clear weather, with no warning.

The role of corporate instinct is to overcome the *long-
term* effects that buried, unexamined memories can have
on an organization by continuously challenging and
replacing past memory. In other words, by resurfacing it
and making it explicit.

RESURFACING BURIED MEMORY

Living beings transfer instinctive behavior from one generation to the next, defying the barriers that seem to prevent
its communication. Animals, however, cannot communicate in complex terms, at least not the way humans do.
Animals should, therefore, have no ability to teach complex
behaviors to their offspring. Yet they do, even the least
complex creatures like insects.

Instinctive actions in animals, are the reflexes that stem
from buried memory. Animals cannot question the current
validity of their buried memory as humans and their organizations can. Therefore, when circumstances change, animals cannot easily change their instincts.

Take migrating birds. Their instinct to fly south is based

on their buried memory that it is cozier down south in the winter. If suddenly an ice age caused glaciers to move into South America, birds could not respond quickly enough to change their destination to a new, warmer climate. Such a response would require genetic reprogramming over a long period of time.

Humans and their organizations can—and must—bring their buried memory to the surface and examine it in the objective light of the present reality.

For example, when Henry Ford built Ford Motor Company, one of his principal concerns was self-sufficiency and bringing as much of the supplier function into the company, so it need not rely on the volatility, reliability, and cost structure of outside suppliers. Ford today realizes it is possible to outsource at competitive prices without compromising the overriding concern about maintaining quality and reliability. The vision hasn't changed, but the corporate memory has had to adapt to a changing market. Many organizations avoid outsourcing and continue to do things on their own, the way they have always done them, despite more effective alternatives. These organizations have become mired in their corporate memory.

Freeway traffic follows a peculiar corollary to corporate memory. Often large stretches of a freeway will stop moving for no apparent reason; drivers encountering the bottleneck will see no incident to cause it. Suddenly, the traffic will ease. This conundrum is, in fact, easy to understand if you observe the freeway from the outset of the bottleneck through its formation. A slight fender bender or a sudden collection of cars that braked as they neared each other causes the problem. Although the incident is eventually resolved, the problem lingers. The congested traffic pattern remains even though the circumstances that created it are constantly being replaced by new circumstances. The traffic pattern formed by the initial event passes its memory of the problem to each subsequent participant until, ultimately, no one in the bottleneck has any first-hand memory of the problem.

The cumulative effect of corporate memory (old ways applied to new markets) can also stall an organization. If every participant in the process could somehow view the pattern from its inception through to the present, the collective understanding would allow the organization, like the traffic, to break free of its artificial constraints.

This is not new thinking, but the technologies to free corporate memory are. As Nonaka Ikujiro claimed in the November-December 1991 issue of the *Harvard Business Review,* a company is "not a machine but a living organism. Much like an individual, it can have a collective sense of identity and fundamental purpose. This is the organizational equivalent of self-knowledge—a shared understanding of what the company stands for, where it is going, what kind of world it wants to live in, and, most important, how to make the world a reality."[1]

The challenge for companies today is to develop corporate instinct to harness the vast collection of knowledge that they have about themselves and their core competencies. They must do this in a timely and meaningful manner, so they can jump on a new market opportunity. Some organizations we studied were, in fact, able to draw on their core competencies even as their products or services were drastically threatened by changing markets. These organizations have the ability to transfer the tacit knowledge of their core competencies across products and people. In this way they overcome the shackles of their corporate memories and cultures. But they are clearly in the minority.

It is often this innate ability to transfer knowledge about an organization's core competencies that eludes most organizations. When core competency exists only in a company's past or is confined in the memory of old experiences and a few individuals, it stymies corporate instinct. Corporate instinct is shared at a much broader level. It arises in memory, but it outlives memory. Instinctive companies are able to see beyond the blinders of past success. As a friend at Arthur D. Little once told us, "I've seen more companies fail because of their success than any other reason." Success tends to create repetitive patterns within the organization under the assumption that repeating the patterns will repeat the success. However, repeating these patterns is as ludicrous and suicidal as using motifs from the 1960s to sell today's fashion, architecture, or television sitcoms. This is not just a figurative example. Longtime ad agencies such as Leo Burnett have lost large customers, including United Airlines, McDonald's, and Miller Brewing to rogue agencies such as Fallon McElligott. Why? As markets transform, so must a business, and its message of transformation must be clear. According to Burnett chairman Rick Fizdale, "They [United] wanted to transform the airline. We still wanted to make ads. We didn't see that their needs had changed. You gotta keep your head in the game."[2]

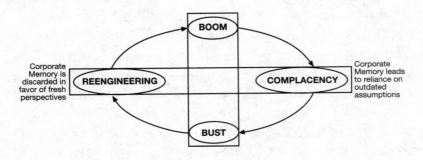

Corporate Memory is discarded in favor of fresh perspectives

BOOM

REENGINEERING

COMPLACENCY

Corporate Memory leads to reliance on outdated assumptions

BUST

Success can easily become the precursor to future failure.

Overt reliance on corporate memory leads to an oscillation between corporate boom and bust. When things are going well, a complacency sets in as people implicitly assume that what worked so well in the past, will work well in the future. But the environment continues to change, and eventually the thinking that proved so successful in the past is wholly inapplicable to the present and future. Only shock tactics like reengineering can break the company free from this thinking. Corporate instinct, on the other hand, avoids this teeter-totter effect by ensuring a constant critical reevaluation of corporate memory, and a careful effort to avoid becoming blinded to the impact of environmental change.

As environments change, organizations must unlearn past behaviors. This seems far too obvious to require pointing out, yet the typical twenty-year corporate *life-cycle* is amazing testimony to the difficulty inherent in this simple proposition. It is no coincidence that patents are granted for seventeen-year periods. In the past, that was the typical life cycle of a product. Today, this is an anachronism in many industries, especially in the field of high-technology where computers, peripherals (printers, scanners, monitors, etc.), and software are obsolete in six-to twelve-month cycles—best case. It's possible for such products to be obsolete before their patents are processed! Take the extreme example of Netscape Communications, the incredibly successful Internet software provider. Netscape provides a ninety-day trial for much of its software, yet it publishes new releases for testing and free download from its Web site on almost a monthly basis. Tapping into new sources of knowledge in these light-speed markets is, therefore, essential to continue the process of innovation at a pace rapid enough to ensure continued survival.

Corporate instinct is an antidote for the chronic syndrome of relying upon past success. When market cycles were measured in decades, or longer, process memory was an important asset. It inculcated a certain procedure and eliminated constant procedural questioning. People who hoped for lifetime employment contracts did little to denigrate process memory. They simply passed it on as unspoken gospel to the next generation of workers. But in today's corporation, if memory cannot be constantly and consistently altered, it is a liability. The problem is not that everything we remember is wrong, but that the inability to question these buried memories assumes that everything we remember is right. In these cases, the corporate memory becomes the water wheel that holds organizations hostage to a single stream of thought.

INCREASING THE SPEED OF INSTINCT

One reason we chose the term *instinct* has to do with the uncanny ability of some organizations to repeat success in ways that defy conventional terms of responsiveness in their industry. These companies persist in coming back—often through innovations that come from the most unpredictable sources and virtually overnight propel them back into the mainstream.

To attribute these innovations simply to the availability of good corporate information or even corporate knowledge is not enough. Most of us would agree that information and knowledge have always been competitive cornerstones of organizations. (You don't need a manifesto on intellectual capital. Just compare the balance sheets and market capitalization of successful high-tech companies). Yet we can't seem to share and leverage information and knowledge quickly enough. We have access to enormous resources of digital information, but today's organizations require much more than the accumulation of information. This information must also be easily organized and distributed according to an organization's changing products, services, and structure.

The greatest obstacle to achieving this nimbleness is the inability to reposition in a new market. However, as we will see in Chapter 6, positioning is a matter of how well an organization adheres to the first rule of corporate instinct: whether it positions itself based on its products or its core competencies. Although traditionally larger organizations have fought desperately to identify themselves through product brands, we will see that *core competency branding* is a far more attractive and preferred approach, and certainly longer lived.

Many high-profile companies are increasingly becoming more and more amorphous in terms of products. Their market position is defined by competency, not by product.

Andy Grove, chairman of computer semiconductor manufacturing giant Intel, is fond of saying that Intel's business is not semiconductors or even software. According to Grove, "We build the guts of modern computing, Period. We'll go away when modern computing goes away."[3]

This sort of positioning also creates soft industry boundaries. Sometimes it's hard to know where one company's industry, such as that of Microsoft, leaves off and that of another, such as that of CNN, begins. This represents a massive convergence of industries, in which a variety of companies in telecommunications, computers, and entertainment are vying to deliver the same products and services to the same markets. However, although different companies are delivering similar products, they do not necessarily have identical core competencies. So Microsoft may try hard with its NBC joint venture, MSNBC, to deliver entertainment, but the jury is still out on whether Microsoft will be able to, or should, extend its core competency to this new market.

Clearly the repositioning of companies is not something new. But the emphasis on competency positioning over product positioning is. And corporate instinct is leveraging the knowledge of core competency in an unlimited variety of products and services—in rapid succession.

IS CORPORATE INSTINCT NEW?

Has corporate instinct always existed? No. What has existed is the instinct of individuals driven by individual vision. To the extent that the vision behind an organization would change often enough for it to recreate itself, the organization had a form of instinct. IBM, for example, literally went through generational shifts in its position, as Thomas Watson was replaced by his son Thomas Watson Jr. Yet these are also examples of glacial change in the vision of the organization. Because of today's extraordinary pace of change the transformations resulting from a strong corporate instinct must occur in spans of time that represent fractions of the product cycles we have become accustomed to over the course of the industrial age.

Unlike the instinct of an individual, which is better described as "vision," corporate instinct can only be leveraged fully when the tools and technologies for its development are readily available. These tools have only recently been developed and are only now being deployed widely. Primarily these are tools for widespread communication and collaboration, inside and outside of organizations. They are tools that more than anything else create self-

knowledge within an organization—what we call a
Knowing Enterprise.

JOINING THE REVOLUTION OF A KNOWING ENTERPRISE

Self-knowledge in an individual builds enlightenment. In
an organization it creates what we call a *knowing enterprise*. But a knowing enterprise, much like Maslow's
enlightened person, cannot simply jump to this stage of
being. It must rely on a foundation of tools and methods
for self-awareness.

When we look back on the second half of this century,
the revolution of self-awareness that led to the adoption of
corporate instinct as a central theme for building successful organizations will clearly be identified as the increasing
momentum toward borderless communications. As
nations, organizations, and individuals have become
increasingly connected, they have begun to traverse the
boundaries that existed during the industrial revolution,
which were so clearly the foundation of traditional organizations. As we look to the next century, the revolution will
be in borderless collaboration. Instead of simply capturing
and transferring individual information, we will be sharing
and leveraging collective learning.

Throughout these revolutions the walls that have stood
between people, departments, divisions, and corporations
will continue to disappear, in no small way due to the evolution of standardized communications technology—from
simple tools such as e-mail and groupware to complex
workflows and intranets.

The result is the evolution of organizations whose
synapses, both internal to the organization and external to
markets and customers, are finally firing in a synchronized

and timely fashion. It is this universal connectivity that is creating the basis for corporate instinct, and in turn is leveraging the intellectual resources and information of organizations in responding to continuously changing market environments.

A knowing enterprise has self-awareness because its technology tools have given it a remarkable capacity to know about itself and its capabilities, resources, competencies, and opportunities.

But this requires letting go of some long-standing assumptions about organizations—what we call "organizational mythology." More specifically, we need to dispel three myths about the enterprise in order to create a knowing enterprise.

- the myth of corporate memory
- the myth of the reactive organization and decentralized decision making
- the mythical team

THE MYTH OF CORPORATE MEMORY

An organization that understands itself and its environment, and responds to the external environment, will be endowed with a very valuable resource—one that cannot easily be replicated by its peers. This is often called a corporate memory. But there is an inherent conflict of objectives when dealing with the capture and perpetuation of *corporate memory.*

There is the danger that instinct provided through a corporate memory can be eroded through attrition. Much of the "instinctiveness" may be captured in the minds of the people in the organization. When they leave, will that instinct leave with them? It would seem, therefore, that one of the key attributes of organizations wishing to develop corporate instinct is strengthening a strong corporate memory. Like instinct in animals, corporate instinct can be passed from generation to generation of employees through memory, even though the generations may not come into direct contact with one another.

However, this may create an enormous liability when people do not question the corporate memory.

An example in the animal kingdom is the annual migration of the herds across Tanzania's Serengeti plains, an event that draws viewers from around the world. During the rain-ripened months early in the year the Serengeti plains are a rich source of food for millions of wildebeest, zebra, eland, and gazelle. As the plain dries during the months of May and June, a collective instinct drives the herds toward sweet grasses of the Masai Mara plains. The migration is called the "Ancient Impulse," due to the massive, nearly simultaneous stampede that occurs. But when the herds gather at the banks of the Mara River, the last natural border to the Masai Mara plains, their instinct for survival plunges them into crocodile-infested waters. Those who make the round-trip crossing with enough strength will return to the Serengeti again in November.

Although one could argue that the value of this collective memory is for the benefit of the species when speaking of the Serengeti herds, the value of an individual in an organization is the contemplation of creative alternatives. When a corporate memory takes over, it eclipses the collective wisdom of individuals. The net liability of a strong corporate memory is that it leads to an unyielding and irrational strategy for the individual. Herein lies the fundamental contradiction between instinct as we commonly know it and corporate instinct. Corporate instinct, unlike animal instinct, is not about creating singular, unyielding, unquestioned drive, but rather creating a constant ability to share the best and newest ideas of an organization.

For example, Apple Computer's obsession with maintaining a proprietary operating environment seemed irrational, long after the market had proven that licensing an operating system was the preferred model. This corporate memory of why Apple had originally succeeded was far too strong for Apple's own good.

Unlike corporate memory, corporate instinct is constantly questioning and adjusting. The organization with corporate instinct is aware of its current capabilities and competencies and applies its internal resources to ever changing external market demands.

THE MYTH OF DECENTRALIZED DECISION MAKING

How is instinctive responsiveness realized in reality? In the human body, many of the fastest (and most valuable) physical responses are called reflex reactions. An electrical shock, for example, stimulates a nerve that sends an impulse to the spinal cord. Unlike many of the body's more conscious responses, however, in a reflex reaction the impulse is sent right back to the shock area in the form of an "impulsive" instruction to act. The response is thus faster and more appropriate to the environmental stimulus than if the nervous impulse had been sent to the rational brain. This is often a productive response, because rational thought would take too long to address the situation. These responses, also referred to as autonomic responses, are a fundamental survival mechanism in humans and animals.

Taiichi Ohno, former Toyota Motor vice president, described this some time ago in the Toyota Production System,[4]

A business organization is like a human body. The human body contains automatic nerves that work without regards for human wishes and motor nerves that react to human command to control muscles. ...

At Toyota, we began to think about how to install an automatic nervous system in our own rapidly growing business organization. In our production plant, an automatic nerve means making judgments autonomously at the lowest possible level; for example, when to stop production, what sequence to follow in making parts, or when overtime is necessary to produce the required amount.

These discussions can be made by factory workers themselves, without having to consult the production control or engineering departments that correspond to the brain in the human body. The plant should be a place where such judgments can be made by workers autonomously.

Although corporate instinct closely approximates the autonomic response Ohno describes, it does not act in the same way in a complex and turbulent business environment that continuously buffets the organization with shocks requiring fast and effective responses.

Continuous reflex reaction is, by its nature, unfiltered and decephalized. In other words, it does not become part of the central intelligence of an organization. It cannot be shared and leveraged by anyone other than the individual or team that is taking the reflex response at that time.

Traditionally, to get around this lack of experiential knowledge, organizations have filtered these environmental conditions up to higher levels, where decisions are made and policies put into place. But this has unfortunate side effects: The process is slow and assumes that senior decision makers are equipped to deal with the problem. Also, lower layers of bureaucracy attenuate the message, so that senior decision makers are unaware of the extent or precise nature of the problem.

Instinctive organizations realize that in addition to the strategic imperatives that management can and ought to drive, there are many other factors that would be faster and more proficiently handled by the people who are in direct contact with the environment. They also realize that the knowledge of these reflexes has value as part of the organization's knowledgebase. This manifests itself as a culture of decentralized decision making across an aware organization.

This does not imply that decision making takes on an anarchic, inconsistent form. Like the human body, the very ability to respond in this way is embedded in the corporate nervous system. Unlike the human reflex, however, a knowledge management system makes this information obvious to the collective organization.

THE MYTHICAL TEAM

One of the most prevalent notions of self-organizing companies is that of teams. The fundamental obstacle to team creation and cohesion, however, is that of team permanency. In a job-for-life work world, teams bonded and created an intense understanding of each others' skills and competencies—to the point that job definitions were irrelevant. Most team management practice has come from this notion of the team. Today, however, teams are more like the cells of a human organ—replacing themselves continuously while the organ as a whole remains functional and intact. Achieving alignment and cohesion in this new work environment requires the equivalent of a corporate DNA that can be shared with each new member of the team. Organizations, like people, are living in constantly changing systems. "Organizations can be thought of as giant organisms with properties like humans," says Helene Uhlfelder. "Teams are microcosms of the organization. Information from chemistry, biology and physics can shed some additional light on what happens with team systems because teams are made up of living systems—people. Our skin falls off and is replaced daily, and every seven years our total blood system is different. Yet we remain ourselves. Team members can come and go from a team, the team changes some, but it remains the same team."[5]

How does corporate instinct make it possible to structure organizations to change at the rapid rate today's markets demand? Where management was once only a function of managing people, today it involves the challenge of managing the intellectual property of people who are constantly moving inside and outside of the enterprise. Management is impossible in this new free-agent work force without new techniques and new technologies like networking.

For instance, corporate knowledge, skills, and experience become far more valuable when shared expeditiously across global networks. You see this more and more in the new breed of executives, chief knowledge officers and chief learning officers, springing up in many companies that are creating knowledge warehouses. These individuals are responsible not just for education and training, but for using information so people can continuously become more aware of their organization's resources.

Consulting firms are an excellent example of the need for managing intellectual assets. John Clippinger, past director of intellectual capital at Coopers & Lybrand, developed one of the industry's leading knowledge repositories to capture and share C&L's vast internal and external sources of information. When fully implemented, the system will provide more than ten thousand worldwide employees with access not only to the information, but more important, the connections between this information that represent the knowledge of the organization.

Corporate instinct is also an organic approach to growing a company. The artificial constructs of hierarchical organizations simply cannot cope or change fast enough to keep pace with the need for innovation at light speed.

In the animal kingdom instincts must change as quickly as environments if a species is to survive. Consider a case presented by D.N. Perkins in *Knowledge as Design*:[6]

Many years ago, a species of white moths frequented a forested area made up of trees with whitish bark. The moths were not exactly the same color. Some were a little darker, some a little lighter. But no moth had a very dark color and most matched fairly well the color of the bark. Birds living in the forest fed upon the moths, albeit with some difficulty since they were nearly invisible in the dark.

The advent of the industrial revolution upset the situation. The soot from nearby factories began to coat the trees... Let us say that 1 is white, 10 is black, and the numbers between measure increasing grayness.

In the first generation of the factories, the moths ranged in color from 1 to 3. But the tree bark had turned a little darker. The birds that fed upon the moths could see the lighter colored moths more easily against the darker bark, and so ate most of them. So the moths left to breed the next generation were mostly 3's. ...

The next generation of moths showed grays 2, 3, and 4. The trees were still getting darker. The birds came and ate mostly the more visible moths of grays 2 and 3, leaving the 4's to breed the next generation.

Again [in] the next generation ... although most of the parents were 4's, the young moths ranged in color from 3 to 5. Again the birds came, eating mostly the 3's and 4's, leaving the 5's to breed the next generation. ...

Gradually, the population became darker and darker, as the birds gobbled up the lighter members of each generation while the darker members remained to breed the next generation. In the course of a few years, the forest was filled with dark moths—moths about the same color as the sooty trees—when originally there had been no dark moths at all.

What is the structure?

This model case illustrates three key principles in the structure of the theory of natural selection. First of all there is *inheritance.* The young moths have more or less the same grayness as their parents. Of course, the principle applies generally to all life: Offspring have more or less the same characteristics as their parents. Secondly, there is *variation.* The offspring of the moths do not always have exactly the same color as the parents, but range somewhat around the parents. In general, the offspring in any species display minor differences from the parents. Finally, there is *selection.* The birds select the lighter colored moths to eat, leaving the darker ones to breed the next generation. In general, it is commonplace in nature that some factor in the environment—a predator, availability of a certain food, temperature, amount of water, and so on—makes a characteristic advantageous for survival and breeding.

The same is true of companies, their markets, economies and competition. By creating corporate instinct, a company can set the stage for *selection* and *inheritance* of its structure, processes, mission, strategy, and tactics even as they constantly change to meet new market demands.

The difference between the genetics of Perkins' forest moths and an organization's genetics is that the organization has the ability to proactively and consciously change its genetic code—certainly at a much faster rate than a biological life form. The critical question becomes whether these organizational changes will happen as a matter of probabilistic or deterministic means. The former makes change a numbers game—a role of the dice—the latter makes it a management exercise. Our belief is that an understanding of the mechanisms and methods by which such change can be accelerated will create new competitive benchmarks for organizational agility.

The advice and examples of this new competitive benchmark provide a prescription for corporate success in the global information age, where innovation and intellectual capital become the greatest competitive weapon and challenge.

INTELLECTUAL CAPITAL: THE CURRENCY OF INSTINCT

For a knowing enterprise, the value of intellectual capital is essential to recognize and to measure. Although intellectual capital has existed since humans have come together to form enterprise structures that have transferable worth, it has only recently become a topic of heated discussion.

Even when intellectual capital is not recognized on a balance sheet or in a financial transaction, it is always part of the long-term valuation of the enterprise. However difficult to measure, when it is continuously replenished and circulated, intellectual capital becomes a critical factor in developing corporate instinct, which is why we need to consider its role.

Perhaps one of the most perceptive statements about the role of intellectual capital was captured in a *Forbes ASAP* article about the value of intellectual capital, where

John Rutledge wrote, "Balance sheets were never intended to measure the value of a company, and they are not used for that purpose by serious investors. At best, balance sheet measures give an investor a rough idea of the value that can be realized by killing a company, breaking it up, and selling it in pieces, and then only after careful scrutiny." Rutledge claims that using a balance sheet as a metric for a company's value is tantamount to measuring the worth of a human being by adding up the value of the chemicals of which he or she is made. However, he is leery of valuing such an intangible commodity as knowledge.[7]

Thomas Stewart, author of *Intellectual Capital: The New Wealth of Organizations* and thought by many to be the most prominent voice in defining the role of intellectual capital in today's organizations, calls intellectual capital "the sum of everything everybody in a company knows that gives it a competitive edge."[8] Without taking anything away from Stewart's work or definition, we believe strongly that creating corporate instinct requires more than just a summation of knowledge—it also relies on the speed of summation.

Given the prior definition, intellectual capital could be said to have greater value to an organization's corporate instinct if it is buried deeply in the company's products. By buried deeply, we mean that the intellectual capital has been reduced to some very basic elements such as ingredients, distribution, and packaging, which do not change. Just the opposite is true. Intellectual capital is not the secret recipe for KFC or Coca Cola. The role of intellectual capital in building corporate instinct is found in the speed with which new knowledge can be created.

This does not dismiss the importance of intellectual capital to industries in which innovation has historically been a slow process. The market value of companies that succeed in the decades to come will be found principally in their intellectual assets: their people and the knowledge these people have about the organization's core competencies. This is as appropriate for low-tech as it is for high-tech organizations. Take two seemingly extreme examples, Nestlé and IBM.

In 1988, Nestlé acquired Rowntree for about twice its market valuation. In 1995, IBM acquired Lotus corporation, also for about twice its market valuation. Rowntree's products were hardly complex—dinner mints and chocolate bars. Lotus's products, however, had high complexity; software, groupware, communications, etc. Although traditional measures of value still don't factor in intellectual capital, these apparently inflated acquisition prices were based on something—we'd argue intellectual capital.

Intellectual capital does not exist purely in the minds of people. It is also in the products, processes, structure, and network of relationships found in an organization. When IBM purchased Lotus, it expected that senior executives would depart, as indeed was soon the case with CEO Jim Manzi and others. But Lotus's value was not simply in the gray matter of one person, or even one hundred people. It was in the branding, reputation, positioning, customers, and momentum of Lotus. These factors were also in the After Eight dinner mints and the Kit-Kat bars of Rowntree.

So why isn't intellectual capital *just* a function of the product? Because products must change rapidly in today's markets. Take, for example, the revolution in the beer industry that has spawned a proliferation of microbrews from leading beer companies such as Miller and Anheuser-Busch. These are not technologically complex products, yet the value of these companies is based on their ability to demonstrate corporate instinct by quickly converting their intellectual capital into *new* products.

Simply put, when intellectual capital stands still, it loses value. An instinctive organization doesn't let that happen—in fact, it can't. In an era of increasing free agency among workers, the imperative to convert ideas into products fast has never been stronger.

Instinctive organizations are constantly transforming their intellectual capital to products and deliverables. In an instinctive organization this happens continuously, across the entire enterprise. That would represent a daunting challenge for large organizations were it not for the right tools. The Boeing 777 is an excellent example of this principle at work. Designed and built entirely through the use of computer-based tools, the 777 is not a single product, according to one senior executive at Boeing, "it is one million objects of intellectual capital flying in close formation." If you are fearful of flying, that may send shivers up your spine as you think of the complexity involved in such coordination. But this is the very essence of good corporate instinct—stitching together the innovative ideas of thousands of people transformed into components that work in an orchestrated fashion. This same coordination used to build the 777 works to build corporate instinct.

These principles have been the same for decades. What has changed when we talk about corporate instinct is not just the importance of capturing good ideas and translating them into products, but rather the tools by which these good ideas can be expeditiously shared, stored, and constantly renewed.

Every organization has intellectual capital. Instinctive organizations leverage it through the use of new technologies and methods that make the intellectual capital tangible by accelerating the velocity of innovation. The faster a company can innovate and convert its intellectual capital to product, the better its corporate instinct and the greater its value.

Accountants, philosophers, economists, stockholders, and business owners have been arguing about how to measure knowledge and intellect. If we persist in focusing on the value of intellect, its value will continue to evade measure. But if we focus on the speed of innovation the intangibility of intellectual assets can be made tangible.

The value of hard goods, such as automobiles, airplanes, and microchips is found principally in the speed with which their intellectual content changes—not in the nuts, bolts, metal, and silicon that make up their parts. Therefore, the degree to which an organization has created accessible and open repositories of intellectual capital and the speed with which it replenishes these will directly affect its valuation in the market. The value of a company in the future will also hinge heavily on the degree to which it can quickly assimilate its intellectual capital with that of other entities. It is this recurring theme of swiftness that creates value from intellect because that is what makes these companies smarter than their competitors. This provides a definitive and tangible benefit when valuing an organization, partnering, acquiring, or being acquired.

Competitive advantage is not only the sum of the intellectual parts; it is the *speed of summation,* or using the vocabulary of corporate instinct, the speed of what we will refer to as the *knowledge chain.* As the pace of innovation, mergers and partnerships, and obsolescence increases, the speed of a company's knowledge chain becomes a benchmark challenge for leveraging intellectual capital into success in all industries.

END NOTES

1. Nonaka, Ikujiro, "The Knowledge-Creating Company," *Harvard Business Review,* November-December 1995. p. 3.

2. "Leo Burnett: Undone by an Upstart," *Fortune,* May 26, 1997.

3. "A Conversation with Andy Grove," *Fortune,* July, 7 1997, p. 186.

4. Ohno, Taiichi, *Toyota Production Systems,* Cambridge, MA: Productivity Press, 1988, p. 45.

5. Uhlfelder, Helene F., Ph.D., "Why Teams Don't Work," *Quality Digest,* June 1994, p. 47.

6. Perkins, D.N., *Knowledge as Design,* Hillsdale, NJ: Lawrence Erlbaum Associates, Publishers, 1986, pp. 15–17.

7. Rutledge, John, "You're a Fool If You Buy Into This," *Forbes ASAP,* April 7, 1997, p. 44.

8. Stewart, Thomas A., *Intellectual Capital: The New Wealth of Organizations,* New York: Currency/ Doubleday, 1997, p. ix.

2

Hooking into the Knowledge Chain

They copied all that they could follow but they couldn't copy my mind, and I left 'em sweating and stealing a year and a half behind.

Rudyard Kipling,
The Mary Gloster

In studying more than 350 companies, a handful of which demonstrated strong corporate instinct, we identified those basic principles of corporate instinct that were strikingly similar among these companies. The most salient characteristic of these companies is the *dynamic adaptability of their people and processes to change ahead of the market*—what we have termed the knowledge chain.

Corporate instinct stems from four definitive stages in the knowledge chain. These are the four building blocks that determine the uniqueness and longevity of any organization. To use the genetic analogy, they are also the factors that allow an instinctive organization to mutate successfully, while extinction claims its competitors. These are the four stages:

- internal awareness
- internal responsiveness
- external responsiveness
- external awareness

The four stages of the knowledge chain define the flow of knowledge through four quadrants, as shown in the following illustration.

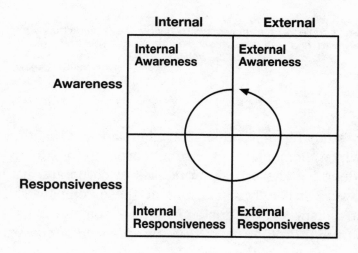

The four quadrants represent an organization's ability to develop fully its internal and external awareness and responsiveness. The counterclockwise circle represents the continuous flow of information within the knowledge chain. In any organization and industry, success is ultimately measured by the ability to best meet the requirements of *external responsiveness*. In each of the cells, however, there are specific tools, methods, organizational structures, and qualities that support or impede external responsiveness.

The cells of organizations with weak corporate instinct look like this:

	Internal	**External**
Awareness	Poor internal awareness is indicated by extensive use of organization charts, management by edict, lack of knowledge sharing, and static policies and procedures.	Protracted customer feedback loops result from belabored market research and a reliance on product branding, rather than competency.
Responsiveness	New ideas are stifled by corporate memory, a hierarchical command and control structure, and extensive departmental organization.	Slow distribution channels result in standardized products, long durations between innovation cycles, and extensive emphasis on internal rate of return.

In organizations with strong corporate instinct all four cells are *permeable,* allowing the immediate transfer of knowledge between the cells. This permeability is the root of corporate instinct. For example, information about the market is translated into new products and services based on the permeability of the top two quadrants.

The cells of organizations with strong corporate instinct look like this:

	Internal	**External**
Awareness	Always collectively aware of its strengths and weaknesses across structural silos and functional boundaries.	Constantly removing filters between the market and its innovative capacity to form true partnerships with prospects and customers.

(continues)

	Internal	**External**
Responsiveness	Able to instantly organize skills based on an unfiltered assessment of the internal awareness of its resources and external market demands/opportunities.	The final measure of instinct as a perpetual ability to meet the market on its own terms—even when the market cannot articulate these and a clear return is not present.

INTERNAL AWARENESS

Corporate instinct is foremost about an organization's ability to understand itself—to have an organizational awareness. It is not only having your house in order, but also knowing what order your house is in. In its simplest terms it is the answer to the question: "What do you do?"

For either an individual or an organization the answer can take two basic forms: *what you make* or *what competencies you use to make it.* For example, an architect's job can be described as either to *design buildings* or to *translate human needs into useful physical structures.* It's a lot easier to say that the architect designs buildings, or more specifically that an industrial architect designs offices or factories. But what happens to the architect if demand for factories and office buildings declines, or even disappears? Internal awareness is answering the question in terms of what competencies the architect has. It is more complex and time consuming, but also more valuable and much more durable. However, this understanding must be an ongoing process since markets will require the products that result from competency to change often and quickly.

There's no point in responding quickly, though, if it's too late. Reengineering, for example, is often little more than overcompensation for a company's initial insensitivity to a market shift. Like the numbed hand placed on a hot stove, such companies may only become aware of the extent of the damage after they smell their own burning flesh. Instinctive organizations, on the other hand, are "wired" with continuous awareness and perception through all levels and functional areas. This enables them to draw much closer to other parts of themselves and, as a result, closer to the market.

Strong emphasis on functional organization structures that often permeates traditional companies inhibits the development of such an internal awareness. Organizations with a rigid functional structure most often define their core competency as their products and services, not their skills. As James Brian Quinn recounts in *Intelligent Enterprise,* "The question usually posed is, 'How can we position our products (or product lines) for competitive advantage?' not, 'What critical skills should we develop to be *best in the world* from our customers' viewpoint?' The former builds current profits, the latter builds long-term preeminence."

It is this long-term preeminence that organizations need most if they are to weather changing markets. But the systems and institutions in place in many organizations undermine this objective. This is especially true in functional organization structures where, as Quinn notes, "each functional group has a psychological and political need to see itself as the company's special source of strategic strength. In neither event are there strong incentives to build the cross-divisional corporate skills that would lead to enterprise preeminence. Corporate effectiveness is undercut to satisfy personal or divisional goals."

Instinctive organizations not only offer incentives for building cross-organizational skill sets, they also make the collective whole aware of these skills, thereby creating high levels of internal awareness.

A knowing enterprise maintains this level of awareness because it always has the knowledge of itself necessary to respond. This is no small feat for typical large organizations that are fragmented, populated by professionals who zealously protect their knowledge, and undercut by information systems that isolate information and prevent collective creation of or access to knowledge.

Creating a knowing enterprise is indeed the principal challenge of corporate instinct. Once the organization has established its own awareness it can proceed to the remainder of the knowledge chain. Until then it is relying far more on the temporal success of its products than on its core skills and competencies.

INTERNAL RESPONSIVENESS

Awareness of an organization's competencies does not, however, guarantee a clear path to successful products or services. An organization may be well aware of its strengths and market demand, yet not be able to adequately effect change within itself quickly enough to meet the market requirement. In our Corporate IQ test, respondents indicated that they had a 30 percent greater external awareness than internal responsiveness. In other words, "we are better at understanding the market than we are at rallying and coordinating our own resources to prepare for a response." No wonder so many of our survey respondents indicated that a good idea had more chance of resulting in a new start-up or ending up at a competitor before their own organization acted on it.

Internal responsiveness considers how quickly competencies can be translated into teams with the skills and

tools to bring a product to market. During the first iteration of the knowledge chain (the knowledge chain is a continuous process) these are almost always small teams of
no more than a dozen or so individuals who collaborate
closely with a beat-the-clock attitude.

In the discussion of organizational structure, we will see
that these small teams are essential to internal responsiveness. Those companies who have adopted such a
structure across their enterprise are what we will refer to
as *federated,* because of their ability to work in alignment
with certain enterprise goals yet move quickly on their
own when new opportunities are uncovered. In our own
research we found that the federated approach was one of
the most likely indicators of long-term success.

EXTERNAL RESPONSIVENESS

An organization's ability to satisfy this cell in the knowledge chain better than its competitors will determine its
success or failure. Instinct is ultimately about the ability to
respond to turbulence outside of the organization by making decisions without having to coordinate and consider all
of the factors in a complex business and market environment. This means that organizations should set their strategy in terms of broad goals and guidelines, and rely on
their ability to "turn on a dime" when the crosshairs of the
organizational environment come into focus with the requirements of the market. This is the essence of corporate
instinct—a level of responsiveness to environmental conditions that is significantly faster and more intelligent than
in the past and than the current competitors.

This is not just serendipity but a prepared organization
ready to strike when it senses opportunity. As Richard G.
Hamermesh notes in *Fad-Free Management,* the pre-

sent-day mantra of "ready, fire, aim" should be a focal point for today's short product cycles. Hamermesh explains that the "smart bombs" used by the military do not require the "ready, aim, fire" approach used in the past.

The smart bomb does not depend on the environmental constraints of gravity and wind but rather on the crew who fires the bomb and then adjusts the trajectory. Aiming is part of the post-decision process—not a prerequisite. This is what we refer to as *post-decision product targeting*— a technique made possible by the advent of technologies such as the Internet, which have the ability to virtually eliminate test marketing. The instinctive organization is, in this regard, as removed from traditional marketing as a Patriot missile is from a Scud—the former has an internal awareness of its target and control over its trajectory; the latter is lobbed at its target, with fingers crossed, like a cannon ball.

EXTERNAL AWARENESS

External awareness represents an organization's ability to understand how the market perceives the value associated with its products and services as well as the changing directions and requirements of its markets. When coupled with internal awareness, external awareness may lead to entirely new markets. For example, when the overnight shipment business began to take off in the mid-1980s, major air carriers recognized an opportunity to couple their awareness of an internal competency to transport objects of any sort with the need for fast same-day package delivery services. The result was a new business that today accounts for a significant revenue stream for many large commercial airlines.

In part, this also goes back to the question of products versus skills. AT&T, for example, ran a series of ads during the mid-1990s showing people using telecommunications to work in all sorts of nontraditional settings—for example, working with their laptops on the beach. The ads were emblazoned with the title, "YOU WILL." They were the brunt of many jokes because they effectively promoted workaholism. AT&T's perception of itself, as portrayed in those ads, was driven by product: extensive visuals of videoconferencing, computer graphics on remote laptops, business around the world, around the clock. But what is AT&T to the market? A source of burden in an already overburdened workforce? Perhaps a truism but not a pretty picture. AT&T is in the business of *bridging time and space* in order to make life easier, not harder. Its current ad campaign looks like anything but a telecommunications revolution. Instead it portrays that competency. In one television spot, set to the soothing tones of Elton John's "Rocket Man," a weary traveler uses an airline phone to meet his wife under the stars on their front porch for a late night rendezvous. The message here, implied subtly, is "YOU WANT," not "YOU WILL." *You will* talks the talk of industrial-age barons who defined their markets. *You want* talks the talk of the externally aware organization that listens to its markets and puts its skills on display rather than its products.

External awareness is not simply a function of extensive focus groups and market research. These often provide false clues. They provide testimony to what the market needs today, or yesterday, rather than what it will need in the future. In the worst case it provides only the answers that the market expects you want to hear. The classic example is that of New Coke, which despite heavy market analysis proved the ultimate folly of most focus groups.

One of the funniest examples of poor external awareness occurred on April 7, 1997, opening day for the
Milwaukee Brewers baseball season. The management of
Milwaukee's stadium had gone all-out to please their fans.
Each eager fan entering the stadium received a commem-
orative baseball. Something to be treasured and passed
down for generations to come. It was not a cheap promotion, but stadium management was sure it was pure marketing genius—a great way to endear loyal fans.

Before the top of the first inning was over, the ball field
became a shooting range. Those treasured mementos
were being dispatched like hail upon the field. Players
became part of a wild arcade game. Three times the game
was stopped. Three times the announcer pleaded with the
fans. Finally, when the ammunition was exhausted, the
game continued.

The idea did not catch on—much to the dismay of fans
in Boston who were already warming up their pitching
arms when word came that baseball's acting commission-
er, Bud Selig, had officially passed a policy against giving
out baseballs to fans—at least until they were on their way
out of the stadium.

Would a focus group that asked fans about the idea of giving out baseballs at the gate, or a test market campaign
where only a few fans were given balls, have resulted in better external awareness? We doubt it. Stadium management
should have known better, but as with so many organizations they regard their customers as a captive audience. If
they don't like the ballpark or the team, they can drive the
three hours to Chicago. These are fans who have lived
through strikes, absurd player contracts, and several less-
than-memorable seasons. Yet they come like the swallows
to Capistrano, year after year, game after game. Few markets are so surely held captive. Unless you own a sanctioned

monopoly (in other words you are immune to the free market), external awareness is not an option.

WHAT REALLY IS EXTERNAL?

One of the peculiarities of the knowledge chain is the way in which we define what is *external*. Given the accelerating use of virtual structures and electronic commerce, the demarcation between internal and external is becoming increasingly more difficult to discern. In the parlance of corporate instinct, the barrier between internal and external awareness is ideally extremely permeable. Understanding this, we can apply the knowledge chain to a variety of organizations inside and outside an enterprise. What is external awareness in one project is internal awareness in another.

For example, the deployment of an information system in an organization requires business analysts to achieve permeability between the IS function and the end users. Analysts must also establish their own internal awareness of IS's core competencies without tying them to a particular technology or software product, since both change rapidly, as do user's demands for both.

3
Learning to Forget*

The greatest difficulty lies not in persuading people to accept new ideas, but in persuading them to abandon old ones.
John Maynard Keynes

MEMORY, KNOWLEDGE, INTELLIGENCE, AND INSTINCT: WHAT'S THE DIFFERENCE?

Faddish approaches may appeal to organizations that struggle with crisis-mode decisions. But crises occur long after the time to take action has expired. These approaches, like the devastating effects of radical medical intervention, may do the job, but as we will see in our discussion about reengineering in Chapter 7, they leave painful scars, even when they do succeed. Corporate instinct is not a fad. It is common sense and common technology tools applied in a consistent framework. *If corporate instinct is radical to an organization contemplating its application, then it is because that organization has not yet faced its crisis.* As Chrysler CEO Bob Eaton said to his board of directors shortly after taking the helm, "My personal ambition is to be the first chairman never to lead a Chrysler comeback." In other words, staying healthy is much easier than getting healthy. Unfortunately, many companies, like many

*Portions of this chapter are reproduced from Koulopoulos, T., "Creating Corporate Instinct," *BusinessWeek,* June 9, 1997.

people, will only invest in their own health care when a grave illness looms.

Richard Hamermesh talks about a call he once received when he was teaching at Harvard Business School, shortly after Tom Peters' and Bob Waterman's *In Search of Excellence* was published. The caller, from a Fortune 100 company, asked Hamermesh if he could help them create a corporate culture.[1] Were it only that easy!

Instinct, as much as culture, is more than information or knowledge management. There are, in fact, some basic differences between these often-confused terms, information management and knowledge management:

> Information management is the *structured organization* of *predefined* data.

> Knowledge management is the ability to *link* structured and unstructured information with the *changing* rules by which people apply it.

But our intent is to go beyond even knowledge management by looking at two additional rungs of this ladder, intelligence and instinct:

> Intelligence or intellect (used interchangeably in our discussion) is the application of knowledge within a specific *known* context.

> Instinct is the *spontaneous* application of acquired and latent intelligence to *unknown* situations with an *unspecified* context.

Lately, organizations have been basing management restructuring on knowledge, as evidenced by the advent and proliferation of the CKO (chief knowledge officer) and the CLO (chief learning officer). However, these are often superficial efforts to link disparate sources of information. Knowledge requires more than the conveyance of information. It must also provide the basis for learning and the compounding of learning—that is, the ability to create longer term intelligence and ultimately what we term "instinctive" behaviors.

In a September-October 1994 *Harvard Business Review* article, Stan Davis and Jim Botkin did a wonderful job of describing the essence of knowledge as the ability to learn from the learned. According to Davis and Botkin, "Whether a piece of music becomes the stuff of knowledge—whether, that is, it enables those who hear it to learn—depends not only on the composition but also on the skill and purpose of the performer. For a beginning pianist, a halting rendition of a waltz can be a learning experience. The same waltz performed by a virtuoso can be a source of knowledge for his or her audience."

Corporate instinct certainly embodies knowledge, but is a significant step beyond knowledge management. Knowledge management is rooted in the idea that mobilizing an organization's intellectual resources is essential in enabling the organization to compete in a world where the previously powerful product differentiators, such as brand loyalty, quality, functionality, and price are now increasingly common. Knowledge management has provided organizations with a way of breaking free from their rigidly held, yet seldom questioned, assumptions about the competitive touchstones of the past, and exposing them to competitiveness based on innovation. Yet knowledge management is only a first step. As the pace of environmental change increases, as competition becomes more intense and the array of technological, financial, and strategic options available to respond to these competitive forces continues to grow, knowledge management will be an insufficient glue to manage this change. Corporate instinct extends knowledge management in two ways.

- It decreases the organization's dependence on its memory of how things were done in the past, and enhances the organization's ability to respond to sudden change.

- It diffuses intelligence from centralized positions of authority across the entire organization, making intelligent responsiveness *universal* within the organization—thus the responsiveness becomes instinctive.

Change in the business environment need not imply that every case or sale in an organization is different from the previous one. In fact, in some of the most rapidly changing industries the processes involved remain consistent from customer to customer. What we mean by environmental change is not the customer-by-customer, day-by-day variations that occur on a microscopic level, but the tectonic shifts occurring on a strategic level—the annulment of previous rules for competition, the evaporation of traditional customer bases, the overturning of technological limitations, and their replacement with completely new markets, products, technologies, and rules for competition.

Twenty years ago the Jeep was a close descendant of the rugged, ubiquitous transport vehicle of the World War II. It was driven in difficult terrain and under extreme conditions, by people who were concerned primarily with functionality and not appearance. Since the 1980s, however, a wave of affluent baby boomers has transformed the rules by which Jeep plays. The car's market changed—

new customers wanted performance, comfort, and aesthetic appeal in a family car that would be driven primarily in an urban environment. The product itself changed—into a luxurious, technologically advanced, high-quality recreational vehicle, and the resulting rules for competing changed. Jeep now has many competitors—even luxury car provider Mercedes—in a sophisticated, high-end market space. Yet from sale to sale, the process of building, marketing, and selling the car remains essentially the same, from car to car.

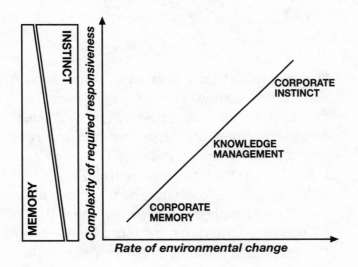

We can visualize the transition from corporate memory to corporate instinct as different levels on a continuum. The graph above shows how the rate of change in an organization's business environment dictates the complexity of responsiveness required. The faster the business environment is changing, the more complex is the responsiveness required of the organization.

This is analogous to the way organisms have evolved in nature. For squids at the bottom of the ocean, the sea temperature and pressure have remained essentially unchanged for thousands of years. Their prey and their predators, too, are the same. As a result, these big animals have a remarkably simple organic structure, yet one that is well suited to the environment in which they live. On the other hand, humans live in a far more aggressive environment. The land is less hospitable than its marine counterpart; conditions can vary widely within days or even hours—weather, vegetation, and topography may change, and (at one stage) wild animals were a constant threat. The human brain was essential in enabling humans to respond effectively to this complex environment.

This complexity of responsiveness is dependent on two factors.

- **The organization's memory.** This refers to the organization's knowledge of, and dependence on, its multitude of past experiences, practices, and attitudes. When an organization's environment changes slowly or not at all, this memory can help it to decide how to approach future problems. However, when the environment is changing rapidly and profoundly, memory may serve to mislead the organization, trapping it into a mode of thinking it believes is applicable, but which in fact does not hold water in the new environment. Thus, the greater the rate of change, the less the organization is able to depend upon its memory.

- **The organization's instinct.** Instinct refers to an organization's ability to create new responses to new circumstances, based not on its memory of the past, but on its ability to understand the causes of current circumstances, and to use its insight and reason in generating the most effective response to them. Instinct is particularly useful where memory

is unsuitable to guide thinking in new circumstances; thus, as the business environment changes
more and more rapidly, so an organization's
reliance on its instinct increases.

We can thus see how the rate of change in an organization's business environment can determine the most
appropriate response to that environment. How do some
organizations handle change more effectively than others?
The secret lies in applying the most suitable response
given the rate of change in the business environment.

CORPORATE MEMORY

When a company exists in an environment that is changing slowly or not at all, the most effective responsiveness
can be achieved by simply applying the same or similar
strategies that were previously applied in the same situation. All the information required to deal with the situation
is at hand; it need merely be extracted and reapplied. As
a result, we speak of memory (or a library of corporate
information) as being the most effective approach.
"Instinct" is not involved at this point, since there is little
decision making to be done. There is a close mapping
between the information required to address the present
situation, and that required in previous situations.
Processes, strategies, and industries that operate at this
end of the knowledge continuum gain no competitive
advantage from the content of their knowledge. As a
result, the driving factors tend to be efficiency and cost.

Corporate memory was widely used as an approach in
the more placid business environment of the past.
Industries evolving slowly were able to dedicate themselves to fine-tuning their products and abilities, safe in
the knowledge that the rules of the game would remain
steadfast. Today, few companies have that assurance, and

thus this approach is applicable to but a small number of companies and industries. Some heavily relationship-oriented industries are still dependent on their corporate memory, such as legal firms—here, the nature of the relationship is key to the product, and is not likely to evolve quickly.

Knowledge Management

When an industry or a company begins to experience change, one of the early warning signs is that the age-old rules that ensured success for so long seem insufficient to stop a gradual slide in profitability. The past becomes less and less of a mirror for the future, and corporate memory as an approach to dealing with the business environment begins to lose its luster. In fact, it may even inhibit an open-minded willingness to consider alternative approaches. However, as long as the pace and extent of change remain moderate, these companies can succeed by using the knowledge garnered in the past as a point of departure for new approaches in the future. Knowledge management is the term given to this decision-making approach, which emphasizes the reuse of previous experiences and practices, with modifications to meet present circumstances. A line of cars, for example, that is no longer selling well may illustrate a shift in consumers' perceptions of the car. While an updated replacement model will need to be technologically and aesthetically more advanced than its predecessor, the manufacturer can rely on some basic truths about the product and its market, truths that have not changed even though consumers' taste for the product has. There is thus a marriage of a knowledge of the past with a fresh approach to the use of that knowledge.

Knowledge management is the force behind the current popularity of knowledgebases—central repositories for an organization's knowledge of its past. Knowledge management, however, implies that this information must constantly be contrasted with that derived from present circumstances, and the gaps filled in by organizational intelligence.

CORPORATE INSTINCT

Knowledge management has enabled companies to respond to the present by making decisions based partly on a knowledge of the past, and partly on a rational analysis of the future. However, in the most rapidly changing environments, where products, markets, and rules change on a month-by-month basis, the intelligence of a centralized group of decision makers may be too slow to translate intention into action, and may thus be as ineffective as no response at all. Huge new markets can be born very quickly and die out as suddenly, especially as the market as a whole becomes saturated with sophisticated products and satisfied needs. We need to be able to decentralize this knowledge, so that its entire force can be drawn upon by nimble teams tasked with meeting a particular challenge. Corporate instinct is the only approach combining intelligence and speed with enough vigor to ensure survival.

Corporate instinct is most effective in industries where rapid, ongoing change is especially common, such as the information technology industry. But it is beginning to spill into other industries. For example, the book-selling industry has been revolutionized by Amazon.com, the Internet-based book retailer, which has completely shattered preconceived ideas about the way in which books are sold, and has set an imperative for other, more established retailers to change their approach.

LEVERAGING KNOWLEDGE MANAGEMENT

Although corporate instinct is the focus of our discussion, knowledge management plays an important role in creating the basis for an instinctive organization. It is worthwhile, therefore, to delve a bit further into how knowledge management supports the concept of corporate instinct.

The information that is used to capture memory accumulates, always increasing. It doesn't regenerate on its own. In fact, when it takes months to sift through, more information can lead to less knowledge. In contrast, you can continually increase knowledge, even with a static information base. Knowledge depends less on the amount of information than on the number of connections that link the information. A knowledgebase allows you to navigate and make sense of these connections easily.

Think of a strand of DNA, the molecule that forms the basis for the genetic encoding that defines the characteristics of every living organism. The complete information store of a DNA molecule is determined by only four bits of data—the molecular basis of thymine, adenine, guanine, and cytosine (TAGC). The information built by these basic elements is a code, unique to specific instructions about the behavior of a cell. The knowledge conveyed through DNA, however, is only evident over time as it is communicated through the behavior of multiple cells in a living organism.

There's a growing realization that knowledge is a factor of production, like land and capital, and that there should be a way to optimize it. But knowledge is a human function. It originates and resides in a human being. In that sense it is a misnomer to say that we can *manage* knowledge. We cannot manage what happens in people's brains, and it's presumptuous to say we can manage people's thought processes. But we can manage how that knowledge is used and we can build systems, tools, and mechanisms to help people better express and thereby share their ideas.

It is perhaps axiomatic that a knowing enterprise is only as effective as the information it learns from is accurate. Information and information systems in a knowing enterprise must be accurate, timely, available to those who need it, and in a format that facilitates their use. In most learning organizations, the tests of information and information systems are simply:

- How does this information add value to the decision process?
- How can it get to the people who need it?[2]

But don't be misled. These organizations do not have the luxury of resting on their laurels. They are constantly challenged by new competitors. Their strength must come from more than a knowledge of what has worked in the past; it must involve the ability to continuously regenerate their knowledge of themselves and their markets. Today's knowing enterprise must regard knowledge as a fragile and volatile asset since it is no less so than the basis of its intellectual capital.

The springboard for the popularity of knowledge management was the painful realization many organizations came to as a result of the massive reengineering initiatives that swept the business world over the past decade. Finally aware of the discontinuity between their environment and their traditional response, these organizations initiated radical initiatives, destroying the implicit repositories of their corporate memory, and rebuilding processes and strategies to address the new environment. While this served to rejuvenate these companies, many made a fatal mistake—they replaced an outdated, invalid corporate memory with a new, soon-to-be invalid corporate memory. Only those organizations able to break free from the shackles of corporate memory altogether, by building a base of corporate intelligence for the future, could be assured that they would not need to repeat reengineering initiatives ad infinitum—or until the company collapsed under the weight of the past.

Many companies today can testify to the fact that they are no longer able to lounge in an industry that is changing slowly or even moderately. Shocking corporate legends illustrate how the once mighty giants of the past have become extinct in the face of a radically changing environment, deposed by smaller, nimbler, smarter competitors. An organization relying on corporate intelligence has reached the stage where its knowledge of the past plays less of a role in guiding its future than its understanding of current circumstances and an innate ability to process and respond to these circumstances. The organization makes a subtle yet profound shift—from relying on its "experience" (or knowledge of the past) to relying on its "skills" (or resourcefulness to handle the future since skills can also become outdated). Knowledge of the past is only valuable inasmuch as it provides a perspective on the future. Skills, on the other hand, equip the organization to respond to as yet unknown forces for change. These skills must include several "metaskills"—skills that enable an individual, and a corporation, to rejuvenate their abilities at critical times; for example, an ability to question assumptions, to learn new techniques, and to thrive in the face of uncertainty.

If we use the term knowledge management, it must be in this context of continuous renewal. We see at least three steps to establishing a knowledge management system that can support such renewal and also provide the cornerstone for corporate instinct. You are unlikely to ever achieve effective knowledge management if you do not first progress beyond each of these:

- knowledge capture
- knowledge inventory
- knowledge transfer

The implication of this hierarchy is that knowledge management does not really exist until a great deal has been done to support it. The term is widely used and widely misunderstood and underestimated. That the foundation of knowledge management requires each of these three prerequisites should be no more intimidating than that an accounting system requires certain generally accepted principles of accounting be followed if it's to be considered reliable.

Understanding each prerequisite provides a sense of how close an organization is to knowledge management and what tools, methods, or cultural issues it must address.

KNOWLEDGE CAPTURE

Far too many organizations focus their efforts on how to get knowledge out of their knowledge management systems and too little, if any, effort acquiring knowledge and getting it into a knowledge management system. The capture and collection of knowledge occurs in every organization without regard to formal mechanisms. But a knowledge management system, like any ecosystem, cannot be constantly depleted of its resource without constant replenishment.

Every organization works with two broad types of knowledge: tacit knowledge that is personal and implicit; and explicit knowledge that is codified and expressed in formal policies, procedures, regulations, and so on. *Tacit* knowledge represents the unique advantage of most small companies or companies in incipient markets where staff turnover is low and informal information sharing occurs naturally between a relatively small group of people. However, there are three obstacles to capturing knowledge:

- *Mobility.* Especially in larger organizations and mature or maturing markets, mobility is the daunting challenge of conveying tacit knowledge as the cerebral assets of the organization when employees and their gray matter are constantly moving in and out of the organization.

- *Half life.* Because tacit knowledge has a limited life span, people who use it should constantly reevaluate the validity of the tacit knowledge on which they base decisions. The problem, though, is that tacit knowledge by definition is not overt or easily accessible. Because it's below the surface, it's not examined often. Individuals may assume that a certain process or business method is correct because it has precedent, even if that precedent is based on outdated knowledge.

  Confusing information with knowledge further exacerbates this phenomenon because we tend to believe that more information creates greater stores of knowledge with which to uniquely differentiate our organizations. In fact, the inverse is true. Greater amounts of information in today's markets tend to level a playing field, since the information is unlikely to be solely available to one organization. Information is simply too easy to replicate and distribute. Knowledge, however, is much harder to replicate outside of an organization's knowledge chain because of the many connections it entails.

- *Threat to specialists.* Many individuals who have become specialists in their areas of expertise are obviously reluctant to part with their knowledge for fear that it will make their skills less valuable.

While the work force is becoming increasingly mobile, not just in terms of geography but more importantly its velocity of change from job to job and company to company, the intellectual value of an organization need not be tied exclusively to the intellectual capital of its workers. This is especially true when you consider the degree to which many market leaders will outsource core business processes to other organizations that are only temporal participants in the intellectual value chain of the organization.

Where then does the intellectual capital lie? The second and third obstacles, *half life* and *threat to specialists,* are based on the fact that knowledge is not a static source—unlike an information base of static contracts, documents, or practices, which can be captured with relative ease. True knowledge is, in large part, found in the sophistication of the methods and attitudes by which that knowledge can be consistently renewed.

What this means is that knowledge cannot be preserved for very long without losing its inherent value—namely, timeliness.

For the insecure knowledge worker, knowledge is only limited power. Of course, the degree of power still depends on the specifics of the industry. The accounting profession changes little in the course of five years, whereas the knowledgebase for engineering and designing integrated circuits changes monthly.

For the organization trying to create a knowledge management system, the challenge is often misstated as simply "knowledge capture" when it is, in fact, "knowledge obsolescence." Having instant access to yesterday's best practices does nothing for a large consultancy like Andersen Consulting if the knowledge is outdated.

Renewing knowledge is much more important—and more difficult—than its simple capture. And doing this stumps most organizations. They realize too late that all their efforts to capture knowledge are nothing more than a casual accumulation of information. Most organizations have been collecting information for some time—but that is not knowledge management.

KNOWLEDGE INVENTORY

Once an organization has mastered the ability to renew knowledge on an ongoing basis, it must find a means of cataloging the knowledge. This, too, appears much easier than it is.

First, because we have become so accustomed to indexing information, in the form of documents, databases, and structured forms, we immediately revert to the same techniques for knowledge. But if knowledge is not information, but the more complex task of making connections between information, consider how much tougher it is to create elaborate hypertext systems of the sort that links documents on the World Wide Web.

These links form the essence of the navigation through a knowledge base, yet they also compound the problem of navigating because they exponentially increase the possible interpretations of any single document. Cataloguing information used to mean searching and finding a set of documents. With knowledge links, any single document can lead to an indeterminate number of other links, making navigation nearly impossible.

In addition, the links themselves must change, as must the documents, if the knowledgebase is to be kept up-to-date. Not only is the job of the knowledge user made more difficult, but the maintenance of the knowledge requires significant added resources.

The only way to resolve this is to rely on intelligent inventory systems that catalog knowledge as it is needed, not in advance. Again, recall that we are not categorizing information that can be stored in predefined categories and standard hierarchies, but instead knowledge that is changing continuously.

KNOWLEDGE TRANSFER

Up until now we have talked about how information needs linkages to be considered knowledge. But both the links and the information need to follow certain rules in order to convey knowledge. In other words, providing a document and a link to two more documents is necessary but not sufficient in conveying knowledge. It is also crucial to convey the *processes* or business rules that govern the use of the knowledge, in order for the information to be transferable to people in the organization.

Consider a salesperson who accesses a knowledgebase to assess the buying habits of a competitor's customer. Numerous documents collected over time reflect prior sales opportunities with the prospect and the history of wins and losses to competition. The history is linked to descriptive information about the prospect's business plans, markets, and strategy. These in turn may be linked to recent market activities that indicate the prospect's success in tapping new opportunities. All of this is important information. Yet can the salesperson readily infer why the prospect might buy from his company, given the current circumstances in the market? With enough time and resource, perhaps.

An alternative would be to bundle certain analytical tools along with the knowledge. For example, a simulation tool could create market profiles based on the current demand for the prospect's products. This tool could create the basis for a business case to buy from the salesperson's company rather than a competitor, perhaps due to an increased ability of the salesperson's company to deliver key support in an area of critical importance to the prospect's current market.

Delivering tools with the knowledge is not far-fetched, especially given the rapid proliferation of the Internet and its ability to deploy small customized applications as part of a typical information transfer.

Knowledge transfer always means transferring the implicit nature of not only *what* but also *how* work is to be done. The latter is a difficult thing to transfer in knowledge work. It is, of course, much easier to transfer the knowledge of how to handle a customer service call at AT&T than it is to train a CEO on how to create a customer service–driven organization.

In summary, most organizations have more knowledge than employees are aware of. Yet most individuals cannot be expected to ask questions about subjects of which they have no knowledge. For example, how does the salesperson in our example know to even perform a market simulation? The solution most organizations turn to is often

training. Not to dismiss the value of training and education, but knowledge transfer presents a much larger problem than training can overcome. When you don't know
what to ask for, all the training in the world will not help.

Information systems put the onus of asking the right
question on the user of the system. Knowledge management systems, correctly implemented, shift that burden to
the system.

At the same time, the knowledge management system
provides users with the ability to expand their understanding of the organization over time, as they discover
new information about their organization that they did not
think to ask.

Having put in place knowledge capture, inventory, and
transfer, a company can truly claim to have developed a
system for knowledge management and in the process laid
a significant cornerstone for creating a knowing and
instinctive organization.

END NOTES

1. Hamermesh, Richard G., *Fad-Free Management: The Six
    Principles That Drive Successful Companies and Their
    Leaders,* Santa Monica: Knowledge Exchange, LLC, 1996,
    p. 7.

2. McGill, Michael E., and Slocum, Jr., John W., *The Smarter
    Organization: How to Build a Business That Learns and
    Adapts to Marketplace Needs,* New York: John Wiley & Sons,
    Inc., 1994, pp. 14–15.

4

The Eight Attitudes
of Instinct

Leadership is practiced not so much in words as in attitude and in actions.

**Harold Geneen,
founder, MCI Communications**

C limbing the ladder from information to knowledge to instinct requires using a set of tools most organizations already own, but rarely use effectively. To use those tools effectively, everyone in the organization must acquire new attitudes and approaches to work. These are what we call the eight attitudes of corporate instinct.

- react before you assimilate

- share—don't impose—knowledge

- become a knowing enterprise

- create process assets

- make instinct transparent

- organize without structure

- decephalize your decision making

- increase velocity and return on time

REACT BEFORE YOU ASSIMILATE

In many sports, players' reactions are determined before they can assimilate all available information. The multiplicity of variables makes it impossible to predict all possible outcomes of an event. This creates a measure of chaos in any sport.

For example, when a professional baseball player swings at a 100-plus-mile-an-hour fast ball, the response is spontaneous, even though the context (is it a curveball, a slider, a change-up) is unspecified. No one really knows what type of pitch is coming next. So why do professional baseball players' batting averages vary widely? For those truly exceptional players, the outcome of the event (hitting the ball) is a given before the pitcher even decides himself what will be thrown. The timeless example, although perhaps more legend than truth, is Babe Ruth standing at home plate before taking a swing and pointing confidently into the distant stands, indicating where he would hit the ball. Arrogant? Perhaps, but with a lifetime batting average of .342, the Babe had great confidence in his instincts—whatever the situation.

In terms of the four levels of responsiveness:

- Information management is the equivalent of any one of us deciding on the right swing given adequate knowledge of baseball and a slow-motion replay of the pitch.

- Knowledge management is the equivalent of a minor league player consistently hitting home runs if he knew the precise style and regimen of the pitcher.

- An intelligent approach is the equivalent of a professional player who understands the type of pitch called for at this point, during the current inning, in this particular game.

- Instinct allows the player to instantaneously react and override all of the above when it comes time to swing the bat. Babe Ruth had instinct.

Although all organizations express some degree of responsiveness at all levels, from information management to instinct, they vary in the degree to which they proactively establish each level as an organizational asset in order to move closer to instinct. It gets harder to capture the myriad skills needed as they climb each rung of the ladder toward instinct. Yet in organizations, and likely in humans, instinct is built on the solid foundation of the other three rungs as a prerequisite. Without a credible approach to managing information, knowledge, and intellectual assets, it is simply not possible to create an instinctive organization—although such an organization may still have an okay batting average, at least compared with a pool of competitors in the same league.

SHARE—DON'T IMPOSE—KNOWLEDGE

Although information and knowledge are basic assets of our organizations, you would be hard-pressed to find a single income statement or balance sheet that lists either, much less one that even acknowledges the existence of corporate instinct. Yet the greatest value of any organization in today's economy comes from these intangibles.

Information stored in a database can clearly be considered an asset. This same information linked together through a series of roles, rules, and process instructions could be considered a knowledge asset.

Instinct, usually reserved for the highest levels of the organization, must not only be part of the organization's fiber and infrastructure, much like a corporate culture, but it must also be conveyed to the organization in overt ways by putting tools in the hands of every employee that permit the organization to share its awareness and responsiveness continuously.

In the case of Digital Equipment Corporation (DEC) during the 1970s and '80s, the tools were lacking, fads were rampant and contradictory, and instinct was reserved for the elite ranks of the organization. DEC held management "woods" retreats (so named because the top management would literally escape to the woods) where DEC executives went to carve out new strategy, which they brought back to the company like the tablets Moses brought down from Mount Sinai. This is not what we are proposing. As with most faddish management techniques, their intent is to reserve instinct for a fortunate few, not to share it but rather to impose it. Imposing any singular strategy over a sufficiently long period of time will defeat the purpose of corporate instinct, which is rapid innovation, by limiting the organization's ability to sense the market with its extremities.

In organizations of this sort, where the instinct is reserved for the higher echelons of the organization, only a radical extrication of top management can turn the organization around, if at all. But this is risky business. Robert Palmer, DEC's CEO since 1992, had to replace Ken Olsen in order for the market, and DEC itself, to renew its faith in DEC's ability to survive. Steve Jobs was ousted to help save Apple, or at least just keep it going. But in these organizations long-term health and prosperity are too tightly linked with the CEO and his or her instincts—again the instincts are not shared. However, playing the game of CEO swapping in order to turn a company around, has a significant downside. This was clearly evident at Apple where a steady succession of CEO's including John Sculley and Gil Amelio seemed only to demonstrate that no amount of savvy or passion could turn Apple around.

In the case of DEC, Palmer's high profile helped to create a sense of short term optimism but his inability to significantly improve DEC's overall performance has driven DEC even deeper into despair. Despite some incredible success with innovations such as AltaVista, a Web-based search engine that receives up to an amazing 30 million hits daily, and a booming service business, Palmer is associated by many with the corporate memory that still ails DEC and has inhibited its growth. The situation is so bad that Geoffrey James, manager of market research at DEC from 1988 to 1994, said in a recent *Upside* magazine article, "The situation [DEC's lackluster performance] will only change when Palmer and Strecker [DEC's VP, Corporate Strategy and Technology], the ultimate architects of Digital's failure, finally step down."[1]

Another example is Michael Eisner, who terrified many Disney stockholders despite his incredible track record at the helm of Disney, because he seemed to hold the lion's share of Disney's instinct.

In each of these situations the CEO was either too tightly controlling corporate instinct or unable to overcome corporate memory. As we will see in our discussion of leadership and corporate instinct, vision has its place, but it cannot provide the long-term direction needed in times of turbulence if it is linked only with one person.

That's the second key criteria for an organization to react to change continuously. It must sense the market with its extremities, not its head. This is what we will refer to as *decephalization*. It is no accident that evolution has put our heads at the far end of harm, or that our most sensitive, agile, and acute sensory nerves are at our extremities, where danger most often meets us. Continuous reaction works when the organization feels with the bottom of the pyramid and not the top.

To have enduring value, corporate instinct must be something deeper than the singular vision of a CEO or *any* single individual. It has to be part of the very genetic makeup of an organization.

Think about companies you know, perhaps even your own, where overrationalization and overanalysis of problems creates competitive obstacles by slowing down decisions and responsiveness.

Even the slowest of these organizations has an imbedded memory, a form of shared understanding about the way things are done, but this is not the instinct we are referring to. It is, instead, a memory that was created for past markets, old economies, and outdated competitive factors.

While organizations are simply a collection of responses to their environment or market, every successful organization attains success by its ability to perceive new opportunity. Opportunity that, although it exists, defies the ability of most organizations to capture it, despite the enormity of great marketing, engineering, and sales forces.

Why? Because large monolithic companies develop corporate memory, which creates filters between the company and the market. These filters do not allow the information that triggers creativity and responsiveness to pass through swiftly enough.

Companies whose instincts have gone stale are like patients with local anesthesia let free to wander through the world. They are rational, coherent, and aware of their predicament, yet numb. They can no longer sense the world around them.

These anesthetizing filters are missing in smaller organizations. As organizations grow, their instincts almost always become stale. The magic is in keeping corporate instinct alive, fresh, and always as agile as the current market.

A strong-willed and visionary CEO may turn an organization around, but effective CEOs such as Lee Iacocca and Jack Welch ultimately create much more than vision. They create organizations that can continue to turn themselves around. In these companies, instinct becomes part of the organization, not just part of a person.

BECOME A KNOWING ENTERPRISE

Although corporate instinct requires a solid foundation of knowledge management, it also differs significantly from much of the current theory surrounding knowledge management, which focuses on explicit knowledge. Corporate "explicit knowledge" is formally expressed in codes of conduct, policies and procedures, and in other documents, manuals, or databases that prescribe corporate behavior. Corporate instinct is found in the way an organization enables the complete knowledge chain of activities it performs. This includes the collective and accumulated experience, skills, and expertise of employees, the information repositories and systems that store the organization's knowledge, and how all of these affect the internal/external awareness/responsiveness of an organization.

Although many corporate information systems managers and consultants have been advocating the benefits of "knowledge management"—gathering and managing intellectual capital that can be leveraged in order to boost productivity and reduce time to market—this focuses only on the internal responsiveness of an organization. It answers the question, "How quickly can I get to existing information if I know what to ask?" but it does not deal well with the unknown, or the classic case of "you don't know what you don't know."

Knowledge and intellectual capital certainly represent one of the modern corporation's most important assets, and interest in the area of knowledge management is bound to keep growing—as it should. By proposing the development of corporate instinct we are not attempting to dismiss the value of good knowledge management. But there is something much more important that has to encompass and govern the knowledge management effort, within a knowledge chain of activities, in order to make the knowledge useful and contemporary—as opposed to limiting and stale, as in the case of the traffic pattern problem we described earlier.

Knowledge management is a valuable exercise that is perhaps long overdue, but it is incomplete as it is usually proposed or described. By the time practices or problems become codified as "knowledge," it is too late to take full advantage of a situation. Also, many knowledge management techniques fail to recognize that a number of basic decisions are—and should be—made at the level of instinct. For example: managers may instinctively modify a manufacturing process to enhance productivity; instinctively reject payment on certain claims; or refuse the request for a loan based not on explicit criteria but according to more tacit, implicit criteria that occur spontaneously. When asked, "What qualities were most important to managing knowledge?" one senior R & D executive at AT&T ranked *taste* as the most important. Taste, he said, was the ability to intuitively sense what technology investments made the most sense. This kind of knowledge eludes recognition, and will be difficult to capture and process. Can the traditional database or data warehouse adequately represent this sort of fuzzy, almost indefinable knowledge that we are describing? Not as they exist today.

The alternative has been to capture this knowledge purely in the gut or intuition of the employee. But this too is faltering as employees are replaced by free agents who consistently take knowledge with them to new jobs and companies. Individual instinct is sufficient only in cases where long-term teams bond and remain constant. That is no longer the case in the vast majority of organizations.

Anecdotal evidence from service companies that have restructured their staffs demonstrate how extensively companies depend upon this level of individual instinct. Insurance companies, for example, which have pared back staffing in their claims departments, have been shocked and dismayed to find that they soon began carelessly over-paying many of their claims. They traced the problem to the departing employees who had developed informal and intuitive methods of screening those claims. These unorthodox methods involving private knowledge and gut feelings went well beyond the stated policies or criteria for determining the legitimacy and size of payments, but they were nevertheless quite valid and effective.

This same basic principle often leads to key competitors in most industries rising from the ranks of employees who once worked for the leader—yet became disgruntled that their instincts were not heard or taken seriously within the successful status quo. This raises the obvious question: Why do more companies continue to spin-off rather than spin-in good ideas?

To a large extent, these employees were making judgments and evaluations based on their intuitive grasp of a process. This capacity was undoubtedly developed over many years of experience but it was not shackled by the collective and stale memory of the larger organization. The organization, however, was shackled (perhaps mana-cled) by its memory of the past. Breaking away was per-

ceived at worst as a threat and at best as a less-than-suffi-
cient opportunity to warrant the cost of investment.

A classic example of instinct breaking these shackles is
the spin-in of the PC group within IBM by separating it
physically as an autonomous unit in Boca Raton, Florida,
during 1980. Had IBM kept the PC group within the inner
enclave of IBM's Armonk, NY, headquarters, it may have
never realized the tremendous success it did. And without
IBM as leverage, Microsoft may have never followed suit.
It would have been a different industry for these players,
and clearly for others such as Apple, Apollo, and Sun.
Desktop computing would no doubt have proliferated, but
not to IBM's advantage.

In retrospect, IBM's decision appears visionary. However, at the time, it was an instinctive move, backed by
minimal market evidence. It was a good idea that needed
the latitude of autonomy. It was certainly much more than
an exercise in knowledge management. IBM's spin-in of
the PC group based on rudimentary market clues (some
would claim in contrast to the market's requirements) is
an exceptional example of corporate instinct at work. (We
call this a spin-in as opposed to a spin-off because IBM
maintained ownership over the principal benefit of the
product, even though it relinquished creative control during the spin-in.) IBM could afford the risk of investing in
the PC even as an extensive skunkworks—and to its credit, did. Ironically, skunkworks is a type of luxury common
among large successful organizations. Unfortunately, corporate memory of past successful markets and products
most often stifles the realization of this advantage.

In the same breath we should note that demonstrating
good corporate instinct in one decision does not guarantee
100 percent accuracy in future decisions. For example,
some would claim that IBM would have been an even bet-

ter example of an instinctive organization had it not let Microsoft run off with the crown jewels to the operating system, namely DOS.

Interestingly, IBM had evaluated a significant equity investment in Microsoft during the 1980s, but believed that the upside was slight compared with IBM's scale. IBM believed the amount of money and research it would have to put into the fledgling Microsoft would have made it a poor investment, at least in the foreseeable future. Why not just spend the same money making its own desktop operating systems? More than a decade later IBM, under new CEO Lou Gerstner, would compensate for its error by purchasing Lotus for $3.5 billion—twice its market value. In an ironic twist, Bill Gates said in *Fortune's* May 26, 1997, issue, "The notion that this was a good business deal for IBM is the silliest thing I've ever heard." It's supremely ironic that Bill Gates is judging IBM's purchase of Lotus in the same shortsighted manner that IBM had once based its decision not to invest in Microsoft. Then again, no organization can have perfect instinct.

Corporate instinct, as with any competitive weapon, is not an exclusive right. Microsoft's knowledge chain was clearly moving much faster than was IBM's. And the speed of the knowledge chain, more than anything else, determines competitive advantage. This, to balance the scales, is the enormous competitive disadvantage of large corporations, which is why they must operate as smaller spin-ins as often as possible—to leverage corporate instinct and avoid paying the high price of acquiring another organization's instincts.

The same theme is today echoed in companies such as DEC, that have been brought back to life by products that have no precedent in the classic setting of a hardware provider. In DEC's case the products are Internet and intranet tools for search and retrieval, namely AltaVista.

A significant shift toward electronic dissemination of products and marketing through the Internet has also lowered the risk inherent in market testing of new products. AltaVista, for example was started as a Web site with no advertising or fanfare. It soon became one of the most visible and talked about products of DEC. Marketing muscle, productization, formation of a spin-in quickly followed. The knowledge chain was in full swing and within a matter of months the product was well on its way to success.

We must acknowledge that managers manage and make decisions not just at a rational level but on an instinctive one, often depending upon clues and hunches. Whether employees are reading process control dials, deciphering computer printouts, or diagnosing a malfunctioning piece of machinery, they rely on clues of which they are only tacitly aware. Unfortunately, problems and environments change far too frequently for this to be reduced to any form of long-term corporate knowledge base, and even when it is, the links to it are often lost.

What must be done to preserve the organization's ability to respond repeatedly to changing market forces is the sharing of tacit knowledge that individuals within an organization are each reacting to in isolation. Put another way:

- When one individual responds in an intuitive fashion, he or she is not expressing corporate instinct

- When many individuals respond based on past memory, they are not expressing corporate instinct

- When many individuals respond based on a collaborative intuition, they are indeed expressing corporate instinct

This third level of sharing tacit knowing constitutes corporate instinct—and represents its greatest challenge. Managers of large organizations may be unaware of the corporation's reliance on this almost primordial level of knowledge as it is happening. But it often becomes painfully evident in its absence—after significant changes such as the shifting around or removal of certain personnel. The new employees who lack experience cannot merely rely on explicit policies and procedures, and they are not savvy enough to look for the right clues and to accomplish the tacit integration of those clues into meaning. This explains why some of the disruptive effects of downsizing have sometimes been concealed and usually unexpected.

Small organizations, on the other hand, are keenly aware of the importance that this collective wisdom plays in their success. They organize themselves—literally—around each other in order to share their tacit knowledge. But as organizations grow, the sharing is replaced by isolation and protectionism. It is at this stage that the risk of losing corporate instinct begins to manifest itself—especially in times of market or economic turbulence.

Some of these concerns were anticipated in Japan when its steel industry began laying off 25 percent of its labor force. Industry leaders recognized that this unprecedented depletion of the labor force would deplete the stock of tacit knowledge as well. As *The Economist* noted on April 20, 1996, "Would there still be enough skilled people around who knew, just by looking at the color of the furnace flame, when to throw in the odd shovel-full of strengthening ingredients?" Thanks to the permanency of the Japanese work force, soft techniques such as "bonding" and "voluntary management" were able to provide a continuity of learning. Japanese steel firms, for instance, encourage "older-younger" bonding whereby senior employees guide novices by passing along various hints and techniques about a particular job. But other industries or corporations (especially those in the United States where free agency is taking center stage) may not be so fortunate.

Even if we agree and appreciate that managers and workers operate instinctually, that doesn't necessarily imply that the *organization* itself has corporate instinct.

At the beginning of the industrial revolution the great German philosopher Friedrich Nietzsche argued that instinct has the power to grasp a more profound comprehension of the truth. It can disclose reality in its most vital and dynamic form and in its deepest dimensions. He claimed that instinct can result in a level of comprehension that is simply not available to science and logic.

In more recent thinking, Sweden-based Skandia's Leif Edvinsson, one of the world's first directors of intellectual capital, has created a taxonomy of intellectual capital that breaks it down into two basic categories: human capital and structural capital. In his book, *Intellectual Capital,* Edvinsson and his co-author, Michael Malone, describe human capital as the collective property of the individuals within an organization. It cannot be owned by the company. Structural capital, on the other hand, is the infrastructure, from patents to systems and customer/supplier relationships that support the people. This can be owned and transferred for value by the company. Edvinsson believes that structural capital is more important. We agree, but the transference of human capital to structural capital is extremely difficult and often slow because of the barriers between the two.

This is why corporate instinct relies so heavily on computer-based technologies such as the Web, which

lower the threshold for testing a new product. Transforming ideas into instinct is a matter of putting ideas into
action as fast as possible. The greatest impediment we
have seen to this is the traditional route of requiring a bul-
let-proof return on investment (ROI) prior to committing
the organization. Most often the organization will also
assign a minimum value to the ROI, or what is referred to
as an internal rate of return (IRR), that must be met in
order to justify investment in the idea. The fallacy in this
approach is it assumes that all good ideas have a demon-
strable rate of return—they do not. In other words, many
new products, from Sony's Walkman to desktop computing, were considered bad ideas from the standpoint of IRR,
given what market conditions were at the time of their
conception. Conventional wisdom saw these as poor
investments, but the instinct of a few key people saw
otherwise.

In the case of Sony, for instance, both the handheld
transistor radio and the now ubiquitous Sony Walkman
were considered *bad* products from a marketing standpoint. In fact, the original pocket-sized transistor radio,
introduced by Sony in 1957 and met with much doubt
from competitors, was a marketing comedy. Sony salespeople actually had to get oversized pockets stitched onto
their shirts to demonstrate the *pocket-sized* dimensions
of the radio. Similarly, the Sony Walkman was expected by
the market to be a flop based on extensive market
research, Despite this, Sony Chairman Akio Morita had
enormous faith in the product. Both innovations are now
outstanding examples of exceptionally visionary thinking.
But the origins of these ideas, and of Sony itself, demonstrate a much deeper principle of success—the very
bedrock of vision—the best ideas cannot be evaluated
because their value is not yet known. When Morita began
Sony (Tokyo Telecommunications Engineering in 1946)

with $25,000 in capital from his father's sake business and then purchased licensing rights to the transistor from Western Electric in 1953 (coincidentally also for $25,000), he made what were considered unworthy, even foolish, investments by the standards of other companies that could have easily eclipsed his efforts. His decisions were not based on extensive market research, or a proven IRR, but on the stuff of instinct.

Yet few would argue that the ideas for most new products exist in many organizations and many minds. How often have you said to yourself, about a successful product, "Of course! I thought of that!" Two things can be done to improve an organization's ability to capitalize on its inherent idea factory and better exercise its corporate instinct: It can increase the investment in ideas that do not demonstrate a sufficient IRR, or it can reduce the threshold of investment. The first is a potluck approach in the hope that out of many new ideas, occasionally a winner will surface. This is the rationale behind many, if not all, of the world's great R&D laboratories, such as AT&T Bell Labs, Batelle, and Xerox PARC. However, this is not a predictable or quick route to success. The latter approach, lowering the threshold, accelerates the knowledge chain and provides a more deterministic approach. This also creates greater structural capital in the organization as it becomes part of a much faster organizational knowledge chain—effectively, a faster assembly line for ideas.

The reason the knowledge chain must be accelerated is that intellectual capital is diminished as the turnover of people increases. In other words, as free agency becomes the norm, the intellectual assets of the organization walk away on a more frequent basis, therefore the need to quickly transform ideas into products. What has been acknowledged by many as the greatest asset of the organization, its people, is more of a liability, as most are merely borrowed for a short duration. In fact, one of Edvinsson's principles is that intellectual capital is a debt, not an asset. According to Edvinsson, "... Intellectual Capital is a debt issue to be regarded in the same way as equity ... it is borrowed from the stakeholders, that is, customers, employees, and so forth."

Human capital will most often evade reduction to rules and, in fact, provide its greatest value when it works outside of the contemporary wisdom. Instead of attempting to reduce it to systems, why not use the structural capital to facilitate the human collaboration of ideas, creativity, and knowledge by allowing structural capital to develop synaptic connections within the organization? Or as Thomas Stewart puts it, "Unleashing the human capital already resident in the organization requires minimizing mindless tasks, meaningless paperwork, unproductive infighting."

In factories workers used manual skills which were finite and could be replaced by machines and automation. In the knowledge enterprise workers rely on intellectual capacity which is limitless and can be expanded far beyond current capacity. But this will require using technology to remove the mundane and monotonous that impedes creative innovation. Corporate instinct leverages and increases human capital; it does not downsize or diminish it.

The knowing enterprise is also one that fully recognizes the critical importance of getting the right information to the right people. Thus, personalized patterns of work and information access will be an essential part of the knowing enterprise. Most corporations inadvertently use an ineffectual "distributorship model" of information dissemination, where information is widely distributed and sent to the worker whether or not he or she needs or wants it.

This indiscriminate diffusion of data has created the familiar phenomenon of information overload.

In stark contrast to this outdated and inefficient model, the knowing enterprise will operate according to a receivership model, enabling people in an organization to tune in to information relevant to them and their work. Quite simply, this novel model reverses the flow of information so that only the information and knowledge necessary for a task is delivered to the worker. It is much more precise than the distributorship approach. As a result, the worker is liberated from the burden of sorting through extraneous information that interferes with responsiveness.

For managers in flat (or flattening) organizations, this technique amounts to nothing less than survival. As the enterprise flattens and layers of management are eliminated, the amount of information directed at remaining managers increases exponentially. But even flat organizations must have the ability to disseminate information through some form of structure. In the absence of hierarchy and its various information filtering mechanisms, the lack of structured dissemination can create sheer anarchy unless a receivership model is put in place.

CREATE PROCESS ASSETS

In the same way new production methods, management science, and technologies made possible the factory automation models of the industrial era, new tools for creating process assets will revolutionize the office of the future. For example, major consulting companies such as Deloitte and Touche, Arthur Andersen, Gemini Consulting, and Price Waterhouse are creating enormous intellectual warehouses of best practices that are instantly accessible to tens of thousands of consultants and analysts around the world. These companies are breaking new ground by capturing and protecting the creative knowledge capital of their organizations. But they are going beyond the basics of knowledge management by tying the knowledge into the specific performance of process tasks. In time these *process assets* will become part of vast repositories of knowledge linked to the how and why of a business. And therein lies one of the greatest strengths of a process asset—its ability to not only capture but preserve for future scrutiny the full rationale and structure of a business process.

The problem, of course, is that most workers are myopic when it comes to comprehending their role in a particular process. Decades of industrial-era mechanization and overemphasis on Adam Smith's once revolutionary idea of the division of labor, which was later implemented widely by General Motor's Alfred Sloan, have led to an overspecialized workforce that often cannot see the forest for the trees. Visualization methods help not only by conveying the role of the individual in the process, but also by delineating the interrelationships of process tasks and the connection between each process and the rest of the organization.

Organizational self-awareness is very much a matter of objectively viewing the organization and its intricacies without relying on assumptions or anachronistic, prescribed practices. But having a true awareness of the enterprise (what we call "process knowing") is hard to come by without true process-rendering technologies, such as modeling, simulation, and visualization discussed further in Chapter 9. The knowing enterprise utilizes specific tools such as visualization (which provide a bird's-eye view of selective processes) that allow virtually everyone in the enterprise to understand processes in their totality and in all their subtleties. This will be critical for representing the instinctual, tacit knowledge of the workers involved in a certain process and leading to the creation of process assets.

Process assets are anything unique to the way organizations run their business—how they educate their sales force to how they build a plane. Nordstrom's personal shoppers, for example, gave it a temporary competitive edge until competitors rallied to try to imitate them. Without staying plugged into the knowledge chain, process assets can become stale or even become liabilities. To remain assets, they must continuously adapt to new industries or new situations. They must be modified to meet the changing and unrelenting demands of customers and markets. Most important, they can become products themselves, which can be sold or licensed to other organizations with similar requirements. Process assets will give entirely new meaning to core competency and competition.

It is crucial to realize, however, that the creation of such a process asset must also include the instinctive, tacit knowledge that contributes to the success of that process. Regardless of how messed up an organization may be, its workers are doing something that is probably not part of the policies or procedures, which could be turned into a process asset, if only the awareness of what was going on existed. Unless the ability to continuously acquire knowledge and translate it into instinct, through the knowledge chain, is incorporated into a process, the processes value will be no greater than an electronic policies and procedures manual.

The concept of tacit knowledge is a difficult one for many people to fully appreciate, in large part because by definition it is inferred or implied by actions rather than explicit rules and statements. Doctors often refer to tacit knowledge as clinical judgment. This is what gives an experienced practitioner the ability to diagnose an illness whose symptoms would befuddle an intern.

Matsushita Electric Company's early attempts to develop a home bread-making machine failed despite extensive research into bread making, including X-rays of kneaded dough from the bread-making machine and bakers. Still, Matsushita was unable to define the mechanics that would govern the correct actions of automated bread making—until it began translating the tacit knowledge of an expert human breadmaker into the explicit instructions of the machine's process. According to Ikujiro Nonaka, who researched Matsushita's efforts, "The Osaka International Hotel had a reputation for making the best bread in Osaka. Why not use it as a model? Tanaka [a programmer for Matshushita] trained with the hotel's head baker to study his kneading technique. She observed that the baker had a distinctive way of stretching the dough. After a year of trial and error, working closely with the project's engineers, Tanaka came up with product specifications— including the addition of special ribs inside the machine— that successfully reproduced the baker's stretching technique and the quality of the bread she had learned to make at the hotel. The result: Matsushita's unique 'twist dough' method and a product that in its first year set a record for sales of a new kitchen appliance."[2]

Ultimately, tacit knowledge can be reduced to a set of rules or converted to explicit knowledge in any given situation, as was the case with the Matsushita bread-making innovation. The challenge, of course, comes when the situations change with greater speed than the ability to translate tacit knowledge into meaningful patterns of explicit knowledge.

INFORMATION ASSETS VERSUS PROCESS ASSETS

Information is typically regarded as one of the key assets in knowledge-creating companies. However, information on its own is insufficient without a context in which to use it. Processes, unlike information, are regularly omitted from the organizational knowledge base. As a result, the "official" process is frequently described in outdated, static, paper-based prescriptions of practice, while the actual process exists only informally in the minds and daily activities of workers. Even if the informal, unofficial process were efficient, it is unsuitable for analysis and improvement. It is also extremely vulnerable to loss of key personnel, who may take unique and valuable process knowledge with them when they leave. When this happens, the organization's practices and eroded core competencies cannot continue to provide a competitive advantage.

Once these processes have been captured as part of a knowledge base, they can be managed far more effectively, and can enable the development of best practices. Processes, which are repositories of corporate intelligence and levers for responsiveness, become key assets for an instinctive organization.

ITT Hartford went so far as to patent its claims-processing activity. Protection such as this was unavailable until recently, because the technologies for work management discussed further in Chapter 9, were unavailable to capture the knowledge of a complex interaction of this type. However, patent protection still relies heavily on an outmoded life-cycle paradigm: It often requires greater time to secure a patent than the useful life of the process asset. Unless patent protection adapts to a framework of continuous, short-lived innovation, the protection of processes in this way are likely to be far less valuable to innovation-intensive industries.

Process assets will eventually create a *living knowledge chain* of competitive assets, which, through the tools and methods we describe in the following chapters, are easily modified as customers and markets change.

MAKE INSTINCT TRANSPARENT

By creating corporate instinct the organization makes its structure transparent to workers—allowing them, and management, to focus on innovation instead of administration. For example, companies like Hewlett-Packard measure success by using innovation benchmarks, which mandate that a certain percentage of profits must come from products that are less than three years old. For these companies innovation is not just a mantra but a way of life.

A well-defined corporate instinct also provides a perpetual model of change, which marries the best of *kaizen* (a Japanese technique of continuous improvement) and reengineering philosophies.

In short, by making the organization's structure *transparent,* and embodying both the explicit and implicit (or tacit) knowledge of workers, the enterprise can respond swiftly without waiting for important information to make its way up the organizational chain of command and through its many obtrusive filters and intermediaries. The more transparent the structure, rules, and processes that govern the enterprise, the more quickly a company can adapt to reflect new circumstances and environmental changes. For example, leveraging corporate knowledge should enable the nimble enterprise to reduce the time to market for new products and to enhance its productivity on a consistent basis.

How does a company achieve such responsiveness and transparency? How does it collect and make accessible the diffuse knowledge of its workers—especially in the face of the formidable psychological challenges implied in this effort? Many employees regard knowledge as their proprietary possession. They fear that once their own know-how or expertise is known by others, they will become expendable. Because information is tantamount to power and job security, many people will not share it easily.[3] However, workers can be motivated to impart and share this information. The corporation must make it clear that workers and managers increase their value and marketability by breaking out of the traditional mode of specialization to become multidisciplinary workers and managers.

Trends in the changing workforce, such as the lack of interest among employers for applicants with career track-records that consist of only a few positions and responsibilities, are resulting in free agents, who are becoming the norm rather than the exception. These individuals typically have a broad range of experience and skills and can even market themselves as small enterprises.

The knowing enterprise is one that has been successful at not only attracting these free agents but also at collecting and making accessible to them its entire stock of intellectual capital: its explicit and implicit know-how about customers, competitors, markets, and manufacturing processes. This data and information must be liberated from various disparate locations such as libraries, computer or paper files, and, above all, the minds of its employees, and it must be integrated into intelligible and coherent patterns of knowledge that can allow the enterprise to be more responsive and agile regardless of the external conditions.

Capturing these patterns of knowledge and transforming them into corporate instinct is the ultimate corporate asset, the unique elements of the knowledge chain that differentiate an enterprise, but more important, allow it to respond quickly to changing markets and competitive forces.

The capture of intellectual capital, especially its tacit or implicit dimension, is a formidable but by no means impossible challenge. In large part the challenge of creating corporate instinct, is showing how the obstacles to collecting this sort of knowledge can be surmounted.

ORGANIZE WITHOUT STRUCTURE

The knowing enterprise uses a fluid organizational structure. Having developed and honed its instinctive power of adaptability through a heightened internal awareness, it will not be locked into petrified organizational arrangements. This is especially evident in the latest organizational mutation of the "virtual organization" whose key feature is its "dynamic switching capability ... its ability to switch to the most cost-effective and efficient means of achieving its objectives."[4]

But the virtual model, as we will see in Chapter 7, can be seriously flawed. If not done thoughtfully, corporations may lose control over important core processes farmed out to suppliers and others. Corporate instinct, by definition, relies on an internal awareness of core competency. Corporate instinct therefore embodies the benefits of virtuality without these risks, as it facilitates dynamic adaptability and enables the enterprise to take the form of different structures based on customer demands of the moment. Hence it is ideally suited for the chaotic demands of today's volatile markets and economy.

DECEPHALIZE DECISION MAKING

Most organizations still cling to a command-and-control model that routes all decisions through a central brain or "head." These organizations are what we term as *cephalic*. When the head is missing, the organization can be said to be *decephalized*. The connotation is that it runs amuck, like the proverbial headless chicken, with no central vision or guiding principles. This sort of chaotic organization has often been referred to as self-organizing, meaning that it responds to the market as it needs to based on its core competencies and resources. Yet if different parts of the organization are disconnected from each other, how can they function in harmony without undermining, alienating, and ultimately competing with each other?

Think of a flock of birds, an ant farm, or even a colony of bees. The organizing principle in these groups is not the "leader" or the "head" but rather a series of decentralized decisions that act off of a common and shared knowledge-base.[5]

While a simplistic metaphor like a flock of birds cannot contemplate all of the complex rules of an organization of humans, the principle of a dynamic distributed organization is germane. The misconception, like that of most theories of organization learning, calls for people to cluster around an organizational leader like moths around a central flame. Although there are species that clearly play a simple game of follow the leader, these are often destructive behaviors in the face of drastic change. The North American buffalo stand is a prime example. The annihilation of buffaloes from the North American plain was in no small part due to a buffalo herd freezing in its tracks when its leader was killed—making the herd a shooting gallery for hunters. The same principle has applied to militaristic institutions, many governments, and certainly traditional organizations. As Vincent Barabba, general manager of corporate strategy and knowledge development at GM, says, "The extent to which command and control is concentrated increases the vulnerability of the entire organization and thereby the imperative to protect it—or, in the case of an enemy, to destroy it or cut it off from its fighting and supporting forces."[6]

Instinctive organizations recognize that people can and want to be free agents, less bound to a central authority. These free agents nevertheless shape the organization according to a synchronized set of guiding principles. They flock around guiding principles rather than the leader—and in the process remain true to their own needs and principles.

The instinctive organization works despite the decephalized nature of its decision making by organizing around its knowledge as a supporting function, rather than being directed by a single leader. Akin to chaos theory—the rules that govern a flock of birds—it is this collective knowing, not the leader, that directs the flock.

In business, we tend to underestimate the ability of people to collectively do the right thing. We often think of mob mentality, where people collectively do the bad thing. On the contrary, in an organizational setting, if you provide people with everything they need to know, they are likely to do the right thing without needing a central leader dictating their every move.

The organizational structure, technology, and philosophy of enterprises that use this framework of corporate instinct allow them to adapt constantly and swiftly to environmental changes. These companies are always prepared to deal with competitive threats and to take advantage of market opportunities.

For example, Andersen Consulting, the IT consulting arm of Arthur Andersen, consists of 30,000 individual consultants organized in small practices, sharing the knowledge of the entire organization. Each practice is run as an individual entity, although all are part of the corporation.

Yet a recent survey conducted by *Consultant News* of more than 40 mid- to large-size consulting companies found that:

- some 60 percent of all firms currently maintain no active best-practices database;

- one out of three consultancies do not use groupware;

- fewer than 25 percent said they presently utilized the much-touted Internet to support a basic range of internal activities like communicating within local or geographically dispersed teams, sending or receiving detailed communications, collaboration on presentations and proposals, or client work and analysis;

- fully a quarter believed that technology provided only somewhat, minimal, or no competitive advantage to their firms.[7]

In the past, organizational structure was the primary mechanism for enabling communication and synchronization of effort. Therefore, the cephalic organization was the only method of communicating common knowledge. However, over the past twenty years, a more efficient and powerful means of meeting these needs has been insinuating itself into our corporate worlds. Information technology now forms the de facto primary method of ensuring cross-organizational communication in many companies that officially still cling to more static methods. Technology has, in fact, begun to play the role previously filled by people on lower levels of the information organization—it is the means of sensing, communicating, and filtering information about the environment, while the people who previously played this part are freed up to become decision makers.

A good example is a typical customer support function. If a customer called, in the absence of technology tools, the customer representative would have to find the customer's file, research the history of what the customer had bought from the organization, and organize all of this into a coherent history before assisting the customer. That would prevent the customer support representative from dealing with the customer's complaint on the spot. If you give the customer support person instantaneous information, he or she can make decisions instead of going through mundane administrative work that puts off the customer. This is clearly not about technology eliminating people, but enabling them to do their job better.

INCREASE VELOCITY AND RETURN ON TIME

The final attitude of the knowing enterprise is its focus on maximizing return on time. ROT is the financial return for a given period of time invested. This is not something that is used in place of return over time or return on investment, both of which are important metrics of an investment's performance. ROI defines the period of time required to recover an investment in a given product. ROT defines the amount of time required to build a product. Another popular way to describe this is concept-to-cash time.

One way to measure ROT is to identify the percentage of revenues or profits generated in any given year by products introduced over the industry's typical product life cycle. This is effectively an innovation quota that defines an organization's ability to keep pace with the market. For example, Hewlett-Packard has historically experienced a 30 percent contribution to its current year revenues from products introduced in the prior three years. This metric accomplishes two objectives. First, assigning such a benchmark for innovation forces the displacement of old ideas and products on a regular basis. Second, the revenue contribution (or profit, if you prefer) forces innovation for value rather than for its own sake. If this appears to be a matter of simple obsolescence, you're right. It is. But it is more specifically a matter of who becomes the "obscelesor" (the one who causes the obsolescence). As we said at the very outset of this book, instinctive companies continuously compete with their own best ideas and make them obsolete, rather than waiting for the competition to do so.

The benefit of corporate instinct is that it reduces the time required to go through a cycle of the knowledge chain and therefore increases the return on time—what you produce over time. ROT provides a basic metric system for measuring how well your knowledge chain works.

Essentially the knowing enterprise will be able to use a concrete set of methods for refocusing on time as the denominator in the return-on-investment equation.

The principal variable in ROT is velocity. This is best illustrated through a simple but often surprising analogy. A lot of people think that a pilot pulling back on the yoke of a plane's controls will increase the plane's altitude. That's a dangerous misconception. In reality, if a pilot just pulls back without increasing power, the plane will stall and fall out of the sky. (To be accurate, the wing stalls by losing lift. However, since it is the wings that keep most planes aloft the result is a falling plane.) The way to go higher is to increase power and speed—that is, velocity. As you slow down a plane, velocity will decrease and it will lose altitude.[8] Similarly, the velocity of an organization's knowledge chain determines its growth potential—the faster the velocity of the knowledge chain, the higher your organization will go.

The faster you go through the knowledge chain, the more "lift" the organization will have and the better its instincts will be. You don't increase instinct by pointing to a marker and deciding that's where you're going. For a short period of time you might go in that direction, but before long you stall, because you haven't created the velocity you need to perpetuate that success.

In other words, for an instinctive organization time becomes the principal unit by which to measure return on investment. Given the necessary pace of change in a globally competitive economy and the rapid obsolescence of new technologies, ROT may well be the key to long-term success and enduring competitive advantage.

END NOTES

1. James, Geoffrey, "Not a Pretty Picture," *Upside,* September 1997, p. 98.

2. Nonaka, Ikujiro, "The Knowledge-Creating Company," *Harvard Business Review,* November/December 1991.

3. For more background on some of these ideas, see Thomas H. Davenport, "Saving IT's Soul: Human-Centered Information Management," *Harvard Business Review,* March-April 1994, pp. 119–131.

4. Spinello, Richard A., "Ethics, Technology and the Workplace," in *Case Studies in Information and Computer Ethics,* Englewood Cliffs, NJ: Prentice-Hall, 1997, p. 240.

5. Resnick, Mitchel, "Changing the Centralized Mind," *Technology Review,* July 1994.

6. Barabba, Vincent P., *Meeting of the Minds: Creating the Market-Based Enterprise,* Boston: Harvard Business School Press, 1995, p. 24.

7. Reimus, B., *Knowledge Sharing Within Manage-ment Consulting Firms,* Fitzwilliam, NH: Kennedy Publications, 1997, p. 1.

8. This example is a simple description of what is actually involved in the principle of "lift." In addition to the variable of "power," a plane's attitude (the degree of inclination relative to the direction of flight), wind speed, wing configuration, and airspeed need to be considered in establishing the actual lift required to keep a plane in flight. By the way, for those who are fascinated by high powered military fighter and attack planes, it is worth noting that the raw power and advanced technology of these aircraft negates most of the theoretical aspects of this discussion. A sudden pull back in these planes can result in the immediate climb of the aircaft.

5

Achieving Dynamic Stability

Coming together is a beginning. Keeping together is a process. Working together is a success.

Henry Ford

The key to the eight attitudes presented in the last chapter is that they enable an organization to react to changes without wasting time by always converting tacit knowledge or clues and hunches into explicit knowledge—by that time it may be too late to correct the problem or take advantage of the opportunity at hand. Organizations that ignore these attitudes do so at the high price of extinction.

Organizations, like a living species, are most responsive to changes in their environments when they react and adapt quickly. These two capabilities, reacting and adapting, are, however, at odds with each other. They create a necessary instability by constantly changing the course of the organization. What made perfect sense yesterday is suddenly out of place. Genetic organisms survive if they can mutate faster than their environments. Organizations survive if they develop habits that do the same. Most important, if instincts are habits, corporations can use the

principles we will describe in this chapter to develop positive and *dynamic* instinct.

Here are the four basic principles of corporate instinct.

- sharing of knowledge
- rogue collaboration
- intelligent autonomy
- unleashing of individual instinct

The product or service of companies that apply these
principles to leverage their corporate instinct may not
necessarily be knowledge. These companies are distinctive in their ability to know enough about their organization, to be *aware* enough of its competencies, and to
reconceive the organization spontaneously and continuously.

Leveraging corporate instinct by applying these principles is best described as creating a *dynamic stability*,[1]
something that is crucial in a fast-paced, technology-
driven, competitive environment. Dynamic stability is a
balance between the instability from sudden changes in
environmental conditions and the actions taken in
response. Another way to say this is that maintaining an
even keel in rough waters requires constant spontaneous
corrections. The result may be gut-wrenching, but it is
necessary.

SHARING KNOWLEDGE: THE *SHARP END* OF INSTINCT

The first step in sharing knowledge is to make the dissemination of existing knowledge as transparent as possible—
so the knowledge itself can become as visible as possible.

This occurs when instincts and tacit knowledge are transplanted from individual employees into short-term institutional memory. The emphasis on *short-term* memory is important since we do not want instinct to become stale in long-term corporate memory. With the help of information technology, various processes and behaviors will become more visible and knowable to others and hence more sharable. The process is what is commonly referred to as *informating*.

As Shoshana Zuboff has observed, to "informate" means to translate and make *visible*. According to Zuboff, "As the information process unfolds, the organization is increasingly imbued with an electronic text that explicitly represents many forms of data which were once implicit, private, or minimally codified. Thus the work environment becomes increasingly 'textualized.'"[2]

However, the term *textualize* is misleading since the connotation is that the process will be written down. This is not the case. In our experience, another policies and procedures manual is the last thing most organizations that are already littered with process descriptions need. Policies and procedures focus on capture and not on the dissemination of knowledge. If dissemination is our objective, then informating must take on the receivership-driven paradigm we introduced in the last chapter. In other words, the dissemination is driven by *only* what the recipient needs to know, not *everything* that is known.

Admittedly, this seems like a contradiction. But if you think back to a point we made very early in the book—knowledge is represented by the links between existing pieces of information—then this makes much more sense. The current links in any knowledgebase reflect how it has been used and therefore the past memory of the organization. This knowledge has value, but corporate instinct is based on the creation of new links and these are created by as yet undefined uses.

For this to work, however, relevant information as well as knowledge must be shared universally throughout the enterprise. According to Peter Drucker:

> Businesses will have to learn that they must build their communications system on information up rather than information down. Information becomes communication only if the recipient understands and accepts it. If information only moves down, that cannot happen. The structure must be based on the upward communication of information that enables those at the top to know what goes on at the bottom, at the sharp end.[3]

The "sharp end," as Drucker calls it, is where knowledge is created and corporate instinct is most pronounced.

ROGUE COLLABORATION

If anything best differentiates corporate instinct from corporate memory, it is the ability to act outside the bounds and bonds of corporate memory on many occasions when new conditions require new innovations in work habits, structure, or the products of an organization. But this requires a highly collaborative culture, while at the same time allowing for a rogue element within the boundaries of collaboration.

This leads to what author Edward Marshall calls "an explicit governance process." According to Marshall, "The rules that govern most work environments are usually unspoken (e.g., 'I won't step on you if you won't step on me;' 'No surprises;' or 'Don't shoot the messenger'). In some companies, there [is] even an unspoken understanding that 'No good deed goes unpunished.' In creating a collaborative culture, the unspoken rules must be made explicit and agreed to by all parties. In a collaborative culture there are no secrets or hidden agendas. This way, people know what is expected of them; they have bought into the agreements and take responsibility for their full implementation."4

In our view, the creation of true corporate instinct builds into an organization's systems and people a greater ability to adapt to volatile circumstances. John Deere, for example, has dramatically shifted away from the term "change management," which implies that change can be managed, formed, and structured to reflect predetermined conditions. Change can at best be prepared for. Change can be anticipated. But it is not predictable. The key here is to create or craft a corporate instinct that is dynamic instead of static, that endows the organization with rapid feedback mechanisms enabling it to react swiftly and nimbly to the changes in its environment, even when conditions take sudden and unexpected turns.

In the context of the knowledge chain, many organizations find themselves in this same predicament when they come to the end of a product life cycle. Ignoring all indications, they rationalize in every possible way why their product is failing due to market conditions. In other words, they reach outside of the internal awareness cell of the knowledge chain and spend all of their time in the external awareness cell, conducting focus groups, market research, and any form of analysis that will ultimately reinforce their position and product. What they should be doing is accepting the clues of the market and reaching internally to build their awareness of their own competencies and responsiveness in order to be able to more readily fly through the problem with a new product or service.

Many of us remember in horrible detail the conclusion of United Airlines flight 232, which lost hydraulic power to its control surfaces and cartwheeled through Gateway Airport, Sioux City, Iowa, on July 19, 1989. What most people do not know is how much worse that airline disaster could have been were it not for the flight crew's ability to draw on the same principle of internal awareness that we have been describing.

When the flight crew of United 232 realized that they had catastrophic failure of their hydraulics, it was apparent that they would have to do something for which there was no written procedure or precedent in commercial aviation. They would need to fly the plane by oscillating power between left and right wing engines to adjust its bank (the degree to which a plane leans from side to side, and turns). To do this they actually recruited an off-duty pilot who happened to be a passenger on the flight. Together, the flight crew improvised a procedure that steered the plane through turns and myriad corrections in flight all the way to a nearly picture-perfect landing. Tragically, a wingtip caught the side of the runway as the plane was landing, sending it into a deadly series of cartwheels. Although 112 passengers perished, it was a miracle that anyone survived, much less the 184 lives that were spared because of the pilot's ability to reach internally for the competencies that were latent in the crew and, amazingly, the passenger pilot.

Were these reactive or proactive actions? We would claim that they were unequivocally proactive responses. The crew did not wait for external conditions to change but instead took full advantage of their ability to apply their knowledge, skills, and competencies in an entirely unconventional situation to go beyond the current procedures of how to do things.

As corporations attempt to develop their own instincts, they must simultaneously make more transparent the internal dynamics of their business, and ensure that the corporate instinct they are creating is more proactive than reactive.

In the *real world*—that is, the world of trial and error, where decisions are measured by their impact not their theoretical merits—instinct results from a steady stream of accumulated wisdom. Corporate instinct is built on a foundation of many tiny mistakes. As odd as that sounds, any significant success requires a great deal of experimentation, failed efforts, skunkworks, and sunken costs. Bill Gates, for example, is said to be investing in no less than 23 separate Internet start-up companies, knowing that not all will succeed, perhaps most will fail, but a few may become stellar performers. There are no guarantees here, only the law of numbers. The more you diversify your bets and the more bets you place, the more likely you are to find a winner. But you can hedge your bets with business simulation and modeling tools that can help determine whether the winners are likely to more than offset the losers.[5]

Simulation and modeling tools allow astute organizations to couple their knowledgebase with variability and predictability (both are a function of any chaotic environment) to determine the probability of likely outcomes. Imagine, for example, that in the United tragedy the flight crew had the ability to enter a simulation mode where they could had foreseen all of the results of their actions. Despite their heroic and incredibly skilled efforts, perhaps they would have done a few things differently. There's not always time in a crisis to do that, but businesses and airlines certainly could simulate potential crisis scenarios as part of training. Reaction time is critical for success. Simulation can enable organizations to develop instinct that can help them avoid the crisis in the first place.

One might say that there are just too many variables involved in most chaotic business scenarios, which makes them impossible to simulate. But the misconception many people have about chaos theory is that it does not have rules and can therefore not be simulated. Just the opposite is true. Chaotic events and organizations follow definite rules and patterns—and these become much more obvious as an organization's internal awareness and responsiveness increase.

As we will see in Part II, these rules can be applied to simulations that *create* new knowledge at a much higher velocity than is possible with a haphazard trial-and-error approach.

Even with the help of sophisticated technologies, however, the capture and creation of corporate instinct will be a formidable challenge. By definition, we are dealing with knowledge that is personal and implicit—hard enough to articulate, let alone compress into digital format. How, then, can it possibly be retrieved from myriad sources, translated into information technology systems, and enhanced to create an instinctual force for rapid change, operative at the corporate level?

As we shall see in the chapters ahead, certain state-of-the-art computer technologies are versatile enough to permit a level of organizational transparency that will allow employees to appreciate the sources of instinctive knowledge within their organizations.

The goal is to use technology to instill "good" habits (collecting information, linking it, and defining ever changing processes) as part of the organizational fabric so that the corporation will act as a unit and make the right decisions without waiting for information to be disseminated throughout the organizational hierarchy, matrix, or team and without the need for long deliberations about the best way to proceed. The right technology can help organizations develop the instantaneous feedback mechanisms that allow the corporation to react more proactively to environmental changes or emerging problems with suppliers and/or customers.

Corporate instinct can do this by allowing the organization to tap the inarticulate, instinctive knowledge of its workers and to channel that knowledge into a positive force that permits flexibility and responsiveness. For any species, whether it be animal or human, the best habits and the highest form of instinctive awareness enable the organism to change and adapt to its environment as rapidly and flexibly as possible. Corporate instinct allows the corporate organism to do the same.

INTELLIGENT AUTONOMY

The mythological King Canute is said to have ruled over his kingdom with an iron rod. But the king was not satisfied controlling just his subjects; he wanted to rule everything. Camping his armies on the sea's edge, he commanded the incoming tide to stop and then recede. Needless to say, the tide did not heed his commands. In spite of the king's furious efforts, the tide drifted imperceptibly in, until the king was engulfed.

How many managers today continue to struggle under the notion that they can still control all the variables governing their organization? We have finally gotten used to the idea that we cannot control the waves of the future, much less see them. We are learning that steadfast attempts to force-fit *external* realities into a perceived view of how things were meant to be simply will not work. While many managers are becoming increasingly aware of this, most are less aware that a parallel exists *inside* the company—that once safe haven where they thought they knew all the variables, and could control each of them.

In a large organization with thousands of employees, hundreds of processes, and dozens of products and projects, it is naive to believe that the organization can be controlled like a puppet on a string. The assumption that the organization is an inherently docile entity that can be controlled is a dangerous illusion. During good times, this leads to a false sense of complacency; when times get tough, and the organization doesn't react quickly and effectively, there is a sense of helplessness.

But the "uncontrollable" nature of the organization need not be a cause for alarm. Some intelligent, yet uncontrolled, forces are at work: the forces of corporate instinct. This instinct can be captured and harnessed to form the basis of an organization's decentralized intelligence.

Previous centuries and the beginning of this one were dominated by a view of workers as interchangeable components that could be designed to work together as part of a large commercial machine.[6] This view is still ingrained in our organizational structure, compensation, and culture. But the emergence of the knowledge economy is causing an increasing dependence on people who are valued not for their hands, but their heads. It is beginning to dawn on organizations that they are staffed by intelligent, free-thinking individuals—people who have a life, an opinion, and a valuable contribution to make.

Managers are starting to accept that one of the most important ingredients in their ability to respond in the future is the intelligence contained within the company's staff. They are also beginning to realize that intelligence undermines efforts to control, let alone fully understand the organization. An organization of cogs and levers could be analyzed and manipulated—a company of independent brains defies analysis and manipulation. The first step in understanding such a company and its responses is to forget notions about the company behaving in a strict cause-effect manner. A more successful approach is to attempt to understand the company's most likely responses, even if these can only be estimated, not measured.

This new way of thinking accepts and respects the "wild" in the company—the source of instinct being those parts of the company that are *not* leashed into a certain approach, but free to respond in ways consistent with, but not predetermined by, the organization's vision.

A company that relies on its corporate instinct accepts that management can neither control nor even predict the outcome of each contingency. Its managers do know that the company is best prepared to handle all contingencies consistent with the company's vision.

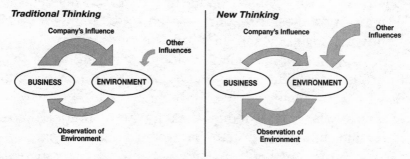

The old paradigm versus the new.

A feedback loop exists between the company and its environment—both external and internal. For generations, managers have assumed that their actions on the environment would dictate the shape of that environment. They would try to control its behavior and had linear expectations of the outcome of their control. However, they are increasingly coming to realize that the environment is highly prone to other influences, and are beginning to accept that its behavior cannot be entirely controlled. Instead, their efforts should concentrate on understanding the environment, and base their expectations on the reality that there will always be uncertainty in the way that the company will respond.

Much of the old thinking entrapping companies is contained in the conventional approach to strategy, which most organizations have used for years. When they talk about strategic formulation, what they mean is a process of building a *machine* that will convert projected opportunities into future business. In this machine view, the organization is armed to fight a particular corporate battle that management sees on the horizon. But it is not always possible to predict what the terms of warfare are going to be until the battle is actually under way.

Corporate instinct, on the other hand, will focus on building the builders—the resources (human, technological and structural) that will, in turn, build the machine—or many machines, if required—each able to convert possibility into reality when the future becomes clearer.

Building a strategic model without knowing what the future holds is akin to building a boat in expectation of a flood—and encountering a drought instead. Instinctive organizations acknowledge that future conditions are uncertain, but believe that the organization can prepare for the future. Instead of building a boat, an instinctive organization protects itself against the weather, whatever it may be—snow, floods, tornadoes, or drought—and then allows *the organization itself* to choose the most effective response when the clouds accumulate.

Few companies today have broken through to intelligent autonomy, at least partially because stockholders don't like the idea that they and their agents may not be completely in control. However, today very few companies are managed by their founders, the people who set the tone for strategy and values in their companies. For those still managed by their founders, fewer still have remained entirely pure to the company's initial central direction. Almost all have undergone some mutation and the influences of others in the company, both past and present. In almost all of these organizations the seeds of corporate instinct remain hidden, dormant, under a thin layer of top-soil waiting for something or someone to awaken them.

Conventional Strategy

Corporate Instinct Strategy

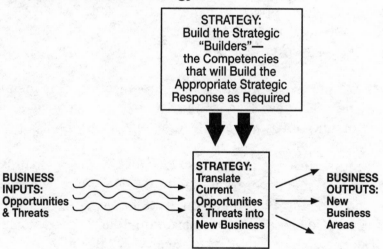

UNLEASHING INDIVIDUAL INSTINCT

Most organizations have some degree of corporate instinct, whether they are aware of it or not. It may take the form of a small group of people who, exasperated by their company's decision making paralysis, have put in place rudimentary systems to ease their work. We worked with a Massachusetts-based probate court registry that had remained in the dark ages of information technology. They had no integrated information systems in place to track important original documents that the public had checked out, including the last will and testaments of Paul Revere and JFK, as well as custody and divorce documents of the general public. Many workers, frustrated with the ineptitude of their tools and the lack of managerial effort to address the situation, had developed an entire manual "infrastructure" to support themselves. These people had exercised their intelligence and expertise to construct fairly sophisticated pockets of intelligence. Of course, their efforts were seriously hampered by a lack of synchronization and synergy with other groups and a lack of technology support. But their efforts demonstrated the basic aptitude and sense of responsibility that the vast majority of workers have—in spite of their organization's ineptitude.

If instinct exists in almost any organization, this means that there are few organizations that cannot consciously develop and nurture it and leverage it as a tool for coping with complexity.

Manufacturing giant John Deere missed an opportunity to leverage its corporate instinct for years—but eventually recognized it. Bill Fulkerson, a staff analyst regarded as an eccentric loner in the organization, toiled anonymously in Deere's engineering labs for nearly two decades, receiving just one promotion over the years. The organization's management simply didn't believe that the mathematician had the wherewithal to be useful, let alone instinctive.

One day, however, looking at Fulkerson's notoriously messy desk, the boss made a comment about a book on the emerging science of chaos theory. Intrigued, Fulkerson began to research the science of complex-systems algorithms research involving genetics. It soon dawned on Fulkerson that these same genetic algorithms

could be used to "breed" the best schedules for construct-
ing planters, the highly customized machines used for
planting seedlings, based on previous schedules. He post-
ed a note on an Internet site where scientists exchange
information about genetic algorithms.

A colleague at a high-tech defense contractor, Bolt
Beranek & Newman Inc., which had used genetic algorithms to schedule work at a U.S. Navy lab, saw
Fulkerson's Internet posting. Keen to make Deere its first
commercial client, Bolt Beranek worked with Fulkerson
on launching a pilot system in 1993 on a PC adjacent to
the loading dock. Within a year, this PC was "breeding"
more than 600,000 schedules every night, each an
improvement over the last. Planters now flow smoothly
through the assembly line and monthly output is up
sharply. Overtime has nearly vanished.[7]

At The Delphi Group, we have been analyzing levels of
instinct inside companies, to see how instinct can awaken
greater external responsiveness. We have administered a
survey called the Corporate IQ Test to executives in 350
companies, polling them on the factors we believe will
drive corporate instinct. We have found no company
devoid of instinct—on the contrary, among the many companies surveyed, a great majority have untapped pools of
intelligence in their organizations. For example, we found
that two-thirds of respondents believed that the dominant
source of intuition in their companies lay outside the management hierarchy. Yet in only 20 percent of the companies are these people involved in strategic decision
making.

Companies have the ability to change their instinct. This
is not an easy process, but there are several techniques
and, as we are about to see, technology tools that can have
a distinct impact on an organization's ability to think
smart, think fast, and think collectively.

END NOTES

1. Our use of this term is from Koulopoulos, T., *Smart Companies, Smart Tools,* New York: Van Nostrand Reinhold, 1997. [Philip Selznick uses a similar term, "dynamic adaptability," but it has a much different connotation. See his *Leadership in Administration* (Evanston, IL: Row Petersen and Company, 1957).]

2. Zuboff, Shoshana, "Informate the Enterprise: An Agenda for the Twenty-First Century," found in James Cash et al. (eds), *Building the Information Age Organization,* Burr Ridge, IL: Richard D. Irwin, Inc., 1994, p. 230. [For a more detailed account, see Shosanna Zuboff, *In the Age of the Smart Machine,* New York: Basic Books, 1989.]

3. Drucker, Peter F., *Managing for the Future: The 1990s and Beyond,* New York: Truman Valley Books/Dutton, 1992, p. 330-331.

4. Marshall, Edward M., *Transforming the Way We Work: The Power of the Collaborative Workplace,* New York: AMACOM. 1995, p. 39.

5. These technologies are discussed further in Chapter 9.

6. Morgan, Gareth, *Images of Organization,* London: Sage Publications, Inc., 1986, pp. 13–17.

7. Petzinger, Jr., T., "At Deere They Know a Mad Scientist May Be a Firm's Biggest Asset," *Wall Street Journal,* July 14, 1995, p. B1.

PART TWO

Managing Corporate Instinct

If one cares about ideas, one wants to gather them from every available source and test them in every possible way.

**Mary Bunting,
Past president, Radcliffe College**

In this section we look at how organizations have begun to sharpen their corporate instinct—and what can be done in your organization. We'll see how the development of corporate instinct relies on four distinct factors:

- building mechanisms to collect, process, and share organizational knowledge on a company-wide level (Chapter 6)

- breaking down organizational structures that have dominated since the beginning of the Industrial Revolution, and replacing them with a new structure (Chapter 7)

- creating a perpetual organization that can quickly take the shape of the market through a federated construct (Chapter 7, 8), balancing internal awareness with internal control

- leveraging a set of technology tools that act as key enablers for the techniques above (Chapter 9)

6

The Velocity of Knowledge

Speed is the only form of security.
John Gage, chief scientist,
Sun Microsystems

As we saw in Chapter 2, the knowledge chain represents the *flow of knowledge and skills* through the organization. The more that knowledge flows through the chain, and the faster it flows, the greater the corporate instinct of the organization.

At any point in time, companies are simultaneously dancing through all four steps of the knowledge chain. In fact, an organization is often at a different level of maturity in each step. However, each time an organization launches a new innovation, enters a new market, or encounters a new development in its industry, it reenters the loop. Ideally, the reentry point will be where external awareness and internal awareness overlap.

For example, just because someone in your organization spots a potential new market for an existing product (external awareness) doesn't mean the company should scurry to serve that market. If the company's core competencies do not align with the opportunity (internal aware-

ness), the new market may not represent such a hot
opportunity. When a new market matches a company's
ability to serve that market—i.e., when internal and external awareness overlap—that triggers a new round of the
knowledge chain that will elevate the company's instinctive ability to respond.

In this chapter we explore how companies can best
accomplish the purpose of each step in the knowledge
chain.

INTERNAL AWARENESS

Internal awareness refers to the organization-wide sharing
of a company's knowledge. This includes its skills, experiences, practices, and the circumstances in which it finds
itself at any given moment. Each part of the organization
has its own particular area of specialty. The aim is for each
business unit to make its unique knowledge more widely
available so that knowledge can assist other business units
in the future.

Internal awareness functions on several levels: to help
the organization develop a perspective on its capabilities;
to create an understanding of its potential capacity; to
make certain skills ubiquitous throughout the organization
and stimulate rapid access to corporate knowledge; to
improve the quality of decentralized decision making; and
to ensure a coordinated strategy across the entire organization.

In the past, organizational structure played the role of
communicating important information throughout the
organization, albeit not very efficiently. The information
changed form when it was handled by layers of bureaucracy that didn't understand it; like the telephone game in
which a message whispered from one person to another in
a sequential chain can change entirely.

Few organizations have put in place the mechanisms and processes for managing the acquisition, screening, and selection of knowledge in even the most knowledge-focused organizations, according to one recent survey.[1] In addition, most of the firms surveyed had no systematic initiatives to measure the impact of these functions.

How do we learn to transfer knowledge in an organization? First, the knowledge must be codified. This means that there must be an understanding of the kinds of knowledge that exist, and where they exist in the organization. A knowledge audit, in which the key categories of knowledge in the organization are associated with specific sources, can accomplish this. It can be done on a broad level—a bird's eye view of the knowledge types and where they reside may be necessary. In a sense, the knowledge audit is aimed at drawing a road map of the knowledge in the organization, identifying the sources of specific technical acumen, which may not correspond to traditional areas of technical or functional specialization. In an organization where different groups may perform multiple functions, there is no longer a clear mapping of abilities. The knowledge audit should also track experience bases, contacts, products, and even new ideas for innovation.

A number of companies and consultants have begun experimenting with ways in which they can measure and taxonomize knowledge. They are assisted by the technology tools used to store and communicate knowledge. For example, by monitoring the access logs of files and documents stored on a file server, a picture of the groups using the information can be obtained. This picture illustrates the way information is actually being used, rather than how it is meant to be used. The information can then be grouped along these access lines, and classified.

Managing the population and design of the knowledge-base should be the responsibility of specific individuals, such as the chief knowledge officer and his or her team, and it must be approached as a dedicated effort.

Captured knowledge can then be recycled. People working on projects and initiatives similar to previous engagements should be able to draw on the knowledge by-products of those previous engagements. This ranges from simple documentation to more complex libraries of research findings. It should also provide the opportunity to combine knowledge from different sources to generate innovative combinations.

There are two approaches to knowledge sharing in an attempt to build internal awareness: the first is preemptive learning, where knowledge is shared in preparation for as yet unknown future circumstances; the second is the use of knowledgeable experts in the organization, who can in a sense consult for the parts of the organization that need a particular form of knowledge.

Preemptive Learning

The first approach to knowledge sharing, preemptive learning, takes the form of longer-term information about generic skills and experiences. Preemptive learning cannot always be customized for a specific project, because the project is not yet known. It is also most suited to high-level knowledge.

Preemptive learning encourages people to share their personal and experience-based knowledge with others. Sharing should optimally be in person, but because face-to-face contact is not always possible or practical in today's distributed organizations, remote communities of practice need to evolve. Communities of practice are groups that form within an organization where people assume roles based on their abilities and skills instead of titles and hierarchical stature.

Notice that we use the term "evolve" rather than "create" when referring to communities of practice. This is essential, as building corporate instinct relies so heavily on discovering new ideas that cannot be predicted or planned for. Evolution is promoted by providing opportunities for informal information sharing throughout the organization. For instance, communications networks and multimedia tools can help convey information, presented in a way that is easy to disseminate and easy to receive by individuals, wherever they may be and whenever they are able to receive it.

IN-HOUSE CONSULTING

When circumstances are more specific, such as when there is a project on the go, knowledge requirements become more focused and answers to specific questions are needed. In these cases, knowledge can rarely be captured with sufficient depth for it to be useful. The most useful approach is usually to track down the source of the knowledge itself, which may be a person or team, a business unit, or a product and its supporting research, documentation, systems, and processes.

Finding this source of knowledge once again requires the use of the knowledge road map that doesn't capture the knowledge itself, but instead provides pointers to the sources of information. Wherever possible, a "live" source should be traced—some person or group involved in the original generation or ongoing use of the knowledge.

Sharing *external* awareness is an important function of *internal* awareness. Because this knowledge must remain relatively current, a form of knowledgebase that is continuously updated is needed because both internal and external factors change continuously. This may mean relaxing required publication standards and providing greater link-age with external parties as knowledge experts.

In the final analysis, internal awareness is as much a function of capturing and regenerating knowledge as it is a matter of retrieving it. This appears to be a subtle point. It is not. Most companies try to achieve internal awareness by focusing on the extraction of knowledge from the knowledgebase, but do little to continuously promote and incentivize the contribution of new knowledge to the knowledgebase.

INCENTIVIZING THE EXCHANGE OF INFORMATION

Capturing knowledge that describes an organization's experiences and practices, particularly if they are new or different, is frequently complex and almost always re-quires much effort—not to mention the significant cultur-al impediments involved. Those who create the knowledge feel little compulsion to record and present this knowl-edge for future use by the organization. After all, those who generate knowledge may be inconvenienced by the need of others to draw on their knowledge. They may already be involved with other projects when previous knowledge they generated is required elsewhere in the organization. And, of course, the knowledge provides them security in their position in the organization.

Nevertheless, such knowledge may prove critical to oth-ers in the organization who may be involved in similar cir-cumstances at a later date. Because the problem is not technical or logistical, but one of motivation, several steps can be taken to improve the willingness of people to cap-ture and share knowledge they generate.

- *Pull knowledge, don't push it.* It will not always prove cost-effective to capture knowledge that may not be reused later. Because it's hard to predict which knowledge may later come in handy, its existence should at least be recorded. Instead of "pushing" knowledge from its creators to as-yet-undefined consumers, the organization can "pull" it by capturing and categorizing indices and pointers to the sources of knowledge, rather than the knowledge itself. This defers the cost of retrieval until the knowledge is actually required.

- *Make the knowledge easier to share.* Existing technology and business systems should be designed with ease of publication in mind. They should be flexible enough to handle many different knowledge sources and formats, and allow knowledge to be used in its existing form as far as possible. Electronic collaboration systems and groupware play a prominent role in easing the burden on the knowledge generator of sharing this knowledge.

- *Reward knowledge sharers.* Some companies are adjusting and reevaluating their performance and compensation review procedures to strengthen the link between knowledge sharing and overall performance.[2] The ultimate value of knowledge derives from its contribution to the value of a finished product. Therefore, a negotiated royalty may be one approach, when it is possible to calculate the value of the final product, or the value added by shared knowledge. Another technique is paying a "knowledge dividend" to each business unit based on the calculation of the overall value of an organization's knowledge assets. This encourages the development of an organization-wide commitment to sharing knowledge, and an awareness of the common benefit which this would bring.

Whatever approach is used, the organization must appreciate fully that the capture of knowledge, especially in an accelerated knowledge chain, must involve the exchange of value for value. In other words, what a knowledge worker imparts to the systems must be at least an even exchange for what they receive in return. Whether monetary, career enhancing, or quality of life, the payback has to be part of the incentive.

INTERNAL RESPONSIVENESS

The organization now has an awareness of the internal environment and has shared this throughout itself, using it to define the company's imperatives and to indicate the areas where the company is to prepare itself. Now the company embarks on the critical task of becoming more instinctive. Internal responsiveness refers to the organization's preparation to go into battle. The desired result is a set of autonomous groups, all of which have knowledge and skill "tool kits" that can be applied wherever they are required. Leadership on all levels becomes a prerogative.

As we will see in Chapter 8, this is where metaskills and federation play the greatest role in the organization's ability to respond.

An example of federation is IBM's mainframe support service. Customers call into a call center, where experts talk them through a process to identify faulty components. The serial numbers of the replacement parts are recorded and reported to FedEx, which warehouses all commonly ordered components at its central hubs. These components have been manufactured by outsourcing partners in

the Pacific Rim. FedEx ships the component to the customer, who is usually able to install the necessary components without assistance. While this is a description of
IBM's mainframe support process, IBM never saw the
hardware, and did not diagnose, manufacture, warehouse,
ship, or install the replacement components. If it had, its
responsiveness would pale in comparison to the speed
with which the current system responds.

The company in this case can be viewed as a series of
smaller organizations with a common mission. Each area
supervisor is an owner of that small company, with the
commitment and savvy to make it work. Finally, each of
these companies is in a partnership with the others, and
their collective victory is a victory for each of them. This
is a prime example of what we will refer to as federation.
It has a collective purpose, shared knowledge, and rapid
velocity.

To hone internal responsiveness, we suggest mastering
three management methods: replicated leadership, the
strategic compass, and continuous reengineering.

REPLICATED LEADERSHIP

Organizations depend on the ability of every business unit
to respond in line with the company's objectives. This can
only be achieved if the thinking driving the organization
has been replicated in each business unit. More than just
the mission and values, each business unit must embody
the same decision making characteristics as senior management. This requires an organization of leaders.

These leaders will not emerge as a result of appoint-
ment to the position. They will naturally migrate into that
role as they become comfortable with the directions,
strategies, and values of the company—in a sense, the
converted become the evangelists for the new creed.

It is thus essential that corporate leadership communicate the most basic tenets, through words and actions. The message to the organization must be: Follow my example, and lead.

United Airlines's chief operating officer and president, John Edwardson, recounts how one of his first tasks in his current position was to sign a memo authorizing the administration department to order $5,000 worth of typing paper. "My first reaction was, 'Is this a test?'" he says. He sent the memo back unsigned, adding that the only thing he would sign was a change to the complex purchasing rules. The second in command of this multibillion-dollar company realized that he had neither the time nor the specific situational expertise to dedicate to such routine tasks, and devolved all responsibility to the departments that dealt directly with the business issues. In doing so, he was teaching the administration department how the organization was led—by its people, not its managers.[3]

THE STRATEGIC COMPASS

At the other end of the federated spectrum, any organization comprising a number of autonomous units each doing its own thing runs the risk of ending up more chaotic than the environment it is responding to. But autonomous units need not, and should not, imply disunity or anarchy. An instinctive organization is guided by a universally embraced strategy that defines its mission, objectives, and values. This strategy then forms a strategic compass, indicating the company's true north. This strategy is developed through the joint decision making of the various business units, and involves a wide cross section of staff to ensure that all organizational knowledge is tapped.

Where there is no need for centralized coordination, each business unit is able to formulate responsive strategy according to the strategic compass.

Here the communications channels of the organization take on new levels of importance. Technology allows all members of the organization to be fully informed of the activities of others. Communication technology also forms a collaborative space within which cross-unit teams can be fleetingly constructed for consulting purposes, before they evaporate.

Management's role becomes one of facilitation. Key support functions remain centralized, but only to ensure economies of scale and of standardization.

CONTINUOUS REENGINEERING

Where traditional reengineering has become a patch-up job for organizations and processes in crisis conditions, corporate instinct prescribes a different approach, both to the motivation for reengineering, and for its execution.

Rather than reengineering to fix inefficient processes, reengineering becomes part of the entire initiative to prevent processes from becoming inefficient in the first place. This calls for a new kind of reengineering—instead of a one-time, top-down effort, reengineering becomes a continuous approach for all in the organization. The people who know the most about a process are the ones who work on it and redesign it as needed. Supported by a new set of technological tools, such as intranets, workflow, process modeling, and simulation, people are able to modify the rules, roles, and routing instructions of the work that they perform. This is backed up by a strategy that governs the guidelines and constraints under which the work can be designed. The result is a constant state-of-the-art process.

EXTERNAL RESPONSIVENESS

Once the organization has prepared itself internally, it is
prepared to swing at the curveballs of the external environment. External responsiveness is about activating the
knowledgebase that has been built up. Finally, the skills
and knowledge tool kits that have been transferred within
the organization enable teams to assemble very quickly in
response to specific environmental imperatives.

There are two aspects to this responsiveness. One is the
cycle of collaborative innovation, which is a continuing
preemptive push toward innovation, and the other is the
rapid-response team, which reacts to shocks from the
environment.

The Cycle of Collaborative Innovation

A continuous process of collective and collaborative creativity and innovation is now possible. External awareness
highlights potential opportunities that can be met by con-
structing the best possible teams from the communities
of practice and core competencies of the organization.
The teams can be multidisciplined, continuously changing
(membership can be fleeting), and are frequently virtual.
Team participants may come from different time zones
around the world.

Collaborative innovation is a systematic cycle of process
execution, knowledge collection, and process refinement.
It is a technique for making innovation continuous.

The Rapid-response Team

Once the teams have been activated, they need to be
deployed quickly and effectively. Much like the original
MinuteMen, soldiers who were trained to be ready to fight
within one minute regardless of the conditions in which

they found themselves, the business units must become prepared to respond immediately. Part of the secret lies in the emphasis on rapid response as a principal measure of success, rather than on costs—what we have already called ROT.

Sun Microsystems teaches a valuable lesson in the art of responding in these new ways. John Gage, chief scientist of Sun Microsystems, believes that the best way to organize 100,000 people is to let them organize themselves. He also believes in harnessing the power of people—whoever and wherever they may be—in support of the company's specific objectives. This is the approach used in the development of the Sun platform-independent programming language, Java.[4]

Java started its life when twenty-five-year-old British programmer, and Sun employee Patrick Naughton, e-mailed Sun's CEO, Scott McNealy, a strongly worded message about why he was planning to leave the company, and how he felt Sun was falling short of its potential.[5] McNealy listened. He initiated a series of internal discussions about what could be done. He took several key developers, including Naughton, and installed them in an office some distance away from the main Sun campus, keeping the operation secret from the entire organization except Sun's senior executives. There was not even a connection to Sun's internal computer network, for fear that the group would be contaminated by a strong anti-innovation faction within Sun. The developers were given carte blanche to translate their ideas into a salable product. A little over a year later, the group demonstrated a revolutionary user interface and programming language for use in almost any electronic device, including home appliances and consumer electronics. But the product stalled, as its developers struggled to find commercial partners, until they noticed the approaching whirlwind of the Internet. The developers realized that their product could have far more significant implications than originally planned. Renaming the programming language Java, they spent six months repackaging Java and releasing it as the platform-independent programming language of the Internet. Today it is the commonly accepted standard for Web programming, and a huge success for Sun. Had Java been developed under the constraints of Sun's traditional corporate structure, had its payback been measured against Sun's standard internal rate of return on hardware, and had the developers not been allowed to operate as an autonomous unit, it is doubtful that Java would have ever become an industry phenomenon. New ideas need independence from the corporate memory, but also support from the corporate vision, in order to reach escape velocity.

But again, the team played by a different set of rules. Rather than publicize the product's benefits by shrouding its internal design in secrecy, the Java team did the opposite. The language was released with little publicity, yet with full details of its design and operation. The old idea was that the only people who could help you invent new things were people inside your company. This seemed to make sense at a time when responsiveness was not affected as severely by external awareness. But Sun realized that external awareness would fuel its ability to respond with yet another fast iteration of the knowledge chain. That was indeed the case. Once the basics of the language and its design principles were published on the Internet, a worldwide team of computer engineering talents spontaneously "volunteered" to pass comments, suggestions, and modifications to the company—in essence, becoming a design and testing force for Sun. Its product was immensely strengthened as a result, but also received favorable publicity and credibility from future users. Most important, it allowed Sun to establish preeminence by developing its competencies faster than any of its competitors. Today, Sun's core competency is providing development tools for the Web—Java just happens to have been the foot in the door, or better yet, the first step into the knowledge chain.

Sun continues to redesign Java—but again, without letting the organization's structure hinder the design process. John Gage notes that his most reliable measure of the organizational influence surrounding Java is the e-mail mailing list of people who form a strategic design task force—from a variety of disciplines, projects, and managerial levels, these people form a virtual but powerful team to guide the development of the product, a team that rarely meets, but is constantly interacting.

Gage attributes the key motivation for these unusual techniques to the great need for responsiveness in Sun's industry. Says Gage, "Speed is the only form of security."

SPINNING IN

Although the knowledge chain is a continuous cycle of internal awareness—internal responsiveness—external responsiveness—external awareness—and back to internal awareness, the cycle will periodically encounter a new opportunity that will require its own chain—as in our example of Java. This area will be different in some way from the usual business—either its markets, the specific skills required, or other factors. In this case, instinctive companies will spin in a venture to attempt to realize the opportunity. Similar to spinning off a successful skunkworks, spinning in keeps the new knowledge chain linked to the organization through a shared internal awareness, ensuring a flow of knowledge between all of the federated units of a business.

Spin-ins are opportunistic. They cannot be designed in; they can merely be identified quickly when they are stumbled upon. In this regard, seeking spin-ins is a process of maximizing the likelihood that they will occur. This requires out-of-bounds thinking and exploration, as well as the sponsorship of senior management. For example, had Scott McNeally not supported the embryonic Java team it is likely that the frustrated team would have left to form its own organization. Such involuntary spin-offs are common in most industries and result in the lion's share of new innovations. Organizations with heightened corporate instinct foster internal innovation.

EXTERNAL AWARENESS

The organization's responsiveness to its business environment will not remain focused for long unless the environment's reaction to the organization's moves are closely observed and internalized. To do this, the organization needs to be externally aware. Your organization inhabits a market space, interacting with customers, partners, and suppliers, influencing and being influenced by environmental conditions. This is the source of the most important information from which the organization will build its knowledgebase.

Through external awareness, the company learns to understand the needs of its customers and the activities of its competitors. This step defines what the company needs to achieve, and the challenges it will face in trying to do so. But as we have already said, this is not simply a matter of conducting extensive focus groups and market research. Opportunity is far too fleeting to allow the luxury of these activities to drive change. Allowing external awareness to filter into the organization means creating sensitized and highly permeable channels for communication with the market.

HARVESTING EXTERNAL KNOWLEDGE

Day after day, a never-ending series of events, activities, shocks, and trends emanate from a company's customers, partners, and competitors, as well as demographic and indirect changes in the market, economy, society, technology, and environment. All these factors provide the company with opportunities and threats.

This requires a radical rethinking of the communications channels we are accustomed to. We may find ourselves talking more to our customers than to people in our company. We may be trading information with our competitors—already a quarter of the companies we have surveyed are doing this. It also requires every person in the organization to become externally aware, not just the marketing and salespeople.

External awareness does not just refer to knowing the customer. Each area of the organization is responsible for researching the external constraints and opportunities that affect it. For example, a major provider of agricultural chemicals stumbled upon a possible innovation in this way. The information systems staff, which collects data about soil conditions as well as possible infestations from plant diseases or insects, was working to develop a technology for gathering information from remote ground-based soil-testing units. They found that ground-based units could be coupled with Landsat photography to determine where possible crop damage might be occurring. This information could then be automatically routed to a distribution facility that would select the appropriate chemicals to treat the problem and ship these directly to the farmer. However, when information systems presented the idea to the R&D group, they received a lukewarm reception, equivalent to "let us handle the business, you handle the computers." The result? The idea ended up being implemented at a competitor before the company could respond.

No one in the organization should confine themselves or others to their silo of functionality. The organization must remove the filters screening people from an acute awareness of the outside world, so they can respond to ideas from far-flung workers—if corporate instinct and the organization is to thrive.

NEW ATTITUDES TOWARD CORPORATE KNOWLEDGE

Knowledge was previously seen as a tool of power and influence to be wielded by the few who possessed it. Today, however, that knowledge is being shared with increasing willingness as people come to realize that the benefits of knowledge are heightened when it is possessed by more—not fewer—people. And sharing knowledge leads to the creation of new knowledge, strengthening not only the organization but the experience of the individuals. This change in attitude has been partially spurred by a new set of corporate communication tools such as intranets and groupware, which are forcing us to change our mindsets and are also showing us the benefits of a less proprietary approach to knowledge.

Sharing with others may seem anathema to many managers schooled in the old "knowledge is power" thinking. Today, managers are recognizing that if the industry grows, we all grow, and that sharing knowledge, even with competitors, can actually result in a win-win situation.

There are at least three techniques companies use to achieve this sharing by broadening their exposure to the external environment:

DISSOLVE COMPANY BOUNDARIES

One of the most important steps in enhancing corporate awareness is an acceptance of the need to break down the boundaries around the corporation. As the limits between what is inside the corporation and what is outside start to blur, far greater chunks of the organization are exposed to the outside world. Some parts of the organization are stretching out to become much closer to the external environment, while at the same time, the outside environment is being granted unprecedented access inside of the company. Already this is a reality, as consultants and contractors take on corporate functions that are increasingly close to the core of the organization.

As we are about to see in the next chapter, new, looser forms of organizational structure are becoming increasingly common. Preferred partnerships, franchise operations, contractors, and consultants are starting to displace the simple unified pyramid that we are so familiar with. These affiliations can be mined for additional knowledge. Involving these external partners in planning sessions, for example, may change the entire perspective of the organization on an issue.

Even in the context of a single federated enterprise this can be a valuable exercise. For example, Masayoshi Son, chairman of Softbank, the world's largest provider of trade shows, has purchased interests in fifty separate Internet companies over the past few years. Knowing that these companies are constantly looking for new ideas, he conducts regular sessions where each CEO of these companies is required to present all innovations and company plans to the other CEOs. The individual companies go off and autonomously develop their own knowledge chains, well aware that not all of them will survive but that this sharing spurs new ideas and innovations. They realize they are all better off for the opportunity to increase their individual likelihood of survival by sharing one ounce of knowledge with forty-nine others. Not a bad deal!

VALUE OUTLIERS

"Outliers" in the company—people and teams that are not tightly bound to centralized company control, and are out there typically dealing with customers or different business environments—may well develop a counterculture because of their different environments. This nurtures an entirely different view of the outside compared to those internally. They may even become extremely close to the customer, so that they become in a sense a customer representative within the company rather than a company representative to the customer. These people, with their different views of the environment, are important players in developing a more complete external awareness, and it is important that their insights be fed to the rest of the organization.

One of the biggest life reinsurers in the United States, whom we worked with, sold more than $40 billion face value worth of reinsurance last year. It accomplished this phenomenal feat with a sales force of two people.

Much of the growth experienced by this company over the last two years has been due to a new business approach. Finding its profits squeezed by the need to undercut competitors' bids, the company began to look at a more value-added, full-service product offering, enabling it to price its products higher. One day while at lunch with an old friend at a client insurance company the marketing manager (essentially a one-person operation handling the East Coast), heard how the client's ability to serve a growing market segment was being constrained by a lack of in-house expertise. Half-jokingly, the marketing manager suggested that the reinsurer create the product for the client, in return for a greater cut of the reinsurance on the product. The client was delighted. Immediately, the marketing manager called upon contacts in the actuarial, underwriting, and marketing divisions of the company, and they set to work designing the client's product. The success of this first deal spurred the marketing manager's colleague in the western region to look for similar opportunities. Within one year, this new "consulting" area became the company's major focus and a significant contributor to the company's future expansion plans.

The marketing manager attributes the success of the venture to the complete autonomy he has to decide which deals to pursue and the attentive ear of management to his need for resources. "It's like running my own company," he said, describing the one-person (now two-person) sales operation, "except I have a set of world-class resources to support me."

We saw this slogan recently on a button distributed to a company's employees: WE ALL SELL. Everyone in the organization has a responsibility to become externally oriented, in all facets of the environment. Corporate instinct cannot be realized unless all people share an appreciation for the needs of customers and for the broad forces driving the business.

BRING CUSTOMERS INSIDE

Allowing the outside world to come in is as important as extending the organization out into the world. From an attitude of shielding the companies' interior from external eyes, there is now much greater openness. Companies are involving customers in product design even more directly by having them perform certain innovation work themselves, for example, becoming involved in customer service or even product design. Nordic Track, for instance, solicits its new product innovations from inventors outside of the company. Even when it comes to competitors, many companies now allow access to internal processes on a reciprocal basis to promote joint learning. Preferred partnerships are setting up what were previously unforeseen levels of cooperation between companies. New levels of on-line connectivity, such as the Internet, intranets, and extranets have enhanced this process.

As the levels of external infiltration into the company increase, greater organizational understanding of external needs and opportunities becomes apparent, and this is then diffused throughout the company much faster than traditional marketing channels have allowed.

END NOTES

1. Reimus, Byron, *Knowledge Sharing within Management Consulting Firms*, Fitzwilliam, NH: Kennedy Publications, 1997.

2. Ibid.

3. Field, D., "United's No. 2 Aims to be Apparent Heir," *USA Today*, July 2, 1997.

4. Rapaport, R., "The Network Is the Company," *Fast-Company*, April/May 1996, p. 116.

5. Bank, D., "The Java Saga," *Wired*, December 1995, p. 166.

7

The Anatomy of
Corporate Instinct

---

*Of all the instincts that the human race is blessed with, none
equals the power of enterprise.*

**Ravindra Chamaria,
Chairperson, Agio Group**

THE DEATH OF THE COMMAND-AND-CONTROL ENTERPRISE

Seventeenth-century British philosopher Francis Bacon is often misquoted as having said, "Knowledge is power." He really said, "For knowledge, too, is itself a power." In the first case the implication is that knowledge makes its holder powerful, in the latter (original quote) the implication is that knowledge is another tool. The way we have distorted his words is a powerful testimonial to the way in which most organizations and individuals perceive the value of knowledge. His intent was not to demonstrate the influence of knowledge as a control mechanism over the worker.

But these good intentions can easily become stymied by the anatomy of a complex command-and-control corporate hierarchy. Like a locomotive, many large, hierarchically managed firms have found it impossible to change the direction of their operations without causing an all-out derailment.

On the other hand, some organizational structures clearly enhance the development of corporate instinct. In our own research we have seen that even a simple application of e-mail, correctly used, can support and promote both high levels of awareness and an acute sense of responsiveness. At Perot Systems, for example, Chairman Mort Myerson is said to run the organization in many ways through e-mail.

To be sure, many companies have already abandoned or modified traditional structures. The driving forces include the availability of new technologies that circumvent or obviate extensive hierarchy and an implicit recognition that hierarchies interfere with swift response to market pressures. This is especially true of the command-and-control enterprise, the hierarchical corporate structure that dominated corporations from the 1950s through the early 1980s.

Annihilating the hierarchy is not the mission of corporate instinct. Mort Myerson does not abdicate his responsibilities of leadership, nor do other successful CEOs. Leadership has value and is imbued with certain strategic instincts. It is the zealous pursuit of such leadership in the absence of corporate instinct that leads to extended hierarchies.

In these organizations the command-and-control message has become a career path more than a structure. As a result, individuals have protected knowledge that could lead to corporate instinct. That is no longer possible, if for no other reason than the availability of so much knowledge in digital form.

In practice, organizational structure is still necessary. What has changed is the rapid restructuring of organizations at many levels into spontaneous micro-organizations.

These micro-organizations are not limited by geography or a stodgy organization chart. They form based on the demands of customers and opportunities, but most importantly they form based on the availability of new technologies that have literally decimated the bureaucratic organization.

The fundamental problem with bureaucracy is that it tends to be *reactive* rather than *proactive*. Its energy is primarily focused inward. It is devoted to developing and refining internal procedures, and, for some clever individuals, to figuring out how to circumvent the rules. Unfortunately, all of this encourages a debilitating insularity. It takes the focus off what is really important: changing circumstances that may present opportunities and threats to the organization's current strategic objectives and plans.

Moreover, the instinctual energy of the organization is sapped by these bureaucratic procedures and tight controls, as employees are persistently discouraged from the free thinking and creativity that is the hallmark of corporate instinct. Bureaucracy tends to perpetuate the worst aspects of corporate memory. When someone questions a bureaucratic policy the response is simply, "That's just the way we've always done things around here"—a devastating attitude when unrelenting market pressures demand a rapid rate of change. In large part, it is this attitude that led to the reengineering revolution of the 1990s.

THE RISE AND FALL OF REENGINEERING

Despite the profound organizational trauma it caused, reengineering was universally embraced for one reason: companies were so desensitized to their environments that only crisis conditions could jolt them into responding—and radical, blank-sheet redesign of processes seemed like the only way they could be made efficient. In a sense, companies were clinging to their corporate memory as a guide for the future—but their corporate memory was obsolete, and was lulling these companies into a false sense of security about their ability to manage in the future.

Reengineering became the final prescription of an industrial age shaped by long product cycles, slow technological obsolescence, and obedient workers. After years of stagnation, reengineering promised drastic action that would catapult corporations to new levels of efficiency. And for a short time this worked.

There is no doubt that the serious inefficiencies embedded in corporate processes warranted a fundamental rethinking of the way they were performed. But reengineering was a remedy for the symptoms of a profound illness. The real problem was (and is) that organizations had become immune to the external and internal forces for change, as the corporate structures and cultures they erected became filters between corporations and their markets.

In a perfect world, reengineering should not have to occur at all. In the real world the degree and frequency of reengineering is at question. With a properly implemented initiative to ensure continuous, people-driven process improvement, extreme forms of reengineering can be avoided altogether.

Instead of infrequent shock treatments, corporate instinct relies on a continuous reevaluation and improvement of business processes, enabled by technology and an empowered, motivated, and knowledgeable workforce.

The term *reengineering* quickly became synonymous with organizational cost cutting and downsizing exercises. Profoundly inefficient organizations, driven by the threat from more efficient competitors with lower cost structures, found it much easier to slash the denominator (cost) of the productivity ratio than to grow the numerator (revenue), to ensure rapid results that would impress shortsighted stockholders and market analysts.

Downsizing actually damages an organization's ability to respond to new opportunities. In fact, the process often leads to "dumbsizing," as the corporation's most talented (and marketable) people seek employment elsewhere.

Cost cutting is by definition finite. The wealth of opportunities open to entrepreneurial companies that focus on numerator management can have an unlimited impact on long-term survival. Seizing these new opportunities requires corporate instinct—which can help a company protect and nurture the knowledge and intelligence embodied in its people and systems.

Hewlett-Packard emphasizes growing the numerator. Its internally imposed "innovation quota" drives it to continually innovate and scour the market for new growth opportunities.

As we mentioned in the discussion about return on time, we should again acknowledge that rampant innovation for its own sake is not the issue here. As Michael Schrage has said, "The innovation issue today isn't, how do I make my innovation better, more valuable, or bring it to market faster? It's, how do we cut our customers' mean time to payback?[1]

Ironically, it is the radical nature of reengineering itself that has contributed most to a shift from employee loyalty to an attitude and work ethic of free agents. The Dilbert cartoons that plaster corporate offices and lunchrooms bear testimony to a workforce that no longer believes in the ability of managers to make ongoing decisions, or even in the concept of "management" as a guiding principal for healthy organizations. If anything is shared among the many jokes, pokes, and jabs at corporate leadership, it is management methods that ultimately hampered organiza-

tions' abilities to leverage their core competencies to innovate and exploit new business areas.

It is clear that corporate instinct can only be liberated in
the organization if people are given the power and tools to
become free agents of change. Managers may continue to
manage, and the need for visionary leadership remains as
strong as always. But management cannot continue to
control all aspects of organizational activity. Processes
must become the property of those who work in them.
This calls for an extension of trust between management
and process workers, which will come when there is clear,
shared understanding of the company's goals and a commitment to providing an environment in which they can be
achieved.

The trauma of reengineering and the bureaucratic organizational hierarchies that necessitated it, offer the best
reason to rethink the very structure of traditional organizations—and to look for alternatives.

UNDERMINING CORPORATE INSTINCT

The dominant management principals of the traditional
bureaucratic hierarchy erode the foundation of corporate
instinct. These include:

- division of labor;
- unity of command;
- authority and responsibility;
- discipline;
- unity of direction;
- order;
- centralization.[2]

While these principles do encourage positive organizational traits such as coordination, corporate coherence, and commitment, they also clearly emphasize command and control, demand discipline and obedience, and impose uniformity. A corporation run according to these principles will not be flexible, open, and adaptive, much less instinctive.

Despite the problems associated with hierarchies, we cannot overlook their benefits. Hierarchies *do* instill a sense of purpose and provide for coordination, drawing their legitimacy from carefully conceived rules and regulations. This creates organizational coherence. In our research we found that an overwhelming number of respondents who work within rigid hierarchies also believe that their organizations are the most "caring." This feeling may not be far removed from the peculiar phenomenon that hostages often feel toward their captors after long periods of captivity. After all, a hierarchy does imply a certain obligation on the part of managers to "take care" of their reports. But it also has serious competitive drawbacks. A key challenge is to find a way to preserve the benefits while eliminating the serious drawbacks.

Hierarchies themselves are not innately perverse or inefficient. Some degree of hierarchy is essential, especially for large, complex organizations. But the principal reason for the hierarchies' domination in the past has been its ability to facilitate complicated patterns of communication throughout the organization. As technology facilitates such communication, it greatly diminishes the need for a complex hierarchy.

The hierarchical model is not dead, its role is changing as market conditions change. According to Brian Arthur, professor of economics and population studies at Stanford, "Hierarchies flatten not because democracy is

suddenly bestowed on the workforce or because computers can cut out much of middle management. They flatten
because, to be effective, the deliverers of the next-thing-
for-the-company need to be organized like commando
units in small teams that report directly to the CEO or to
the board. Such people need free rein. The company's
future survival depends upon them."[3]

But to be truly effective the management *style* of this
modified hierarchy must also be vastly different from the
traditional command-and-control enterprise. Knowledge
must permeate the organization more rapidly and effectively; communications must be more fluid and open, and
workers must become more versatile. Only in a hierarchy
where knowledge and responsibility are decentralized can
genuine anticipatory corporate instinct thrive and make
an impact.

THE EVOLUTION OF ORGANIZATIONAL STRUCTURE

Even in the era of the hierarchical bureaucracy many managers, such as Alfred Sloan, the successful president
(1923–1937) and chairman (1937–1950) of General
Motors, were keenly aware of the virtues of decentralization and autonomy. In his seminal work, *My Years with
General Motors*, he advocates a management style of
"decentralization with coordinated control." Sloan's
description of this model has not lost its relevance:

> From decentralization we get initiative, responsibility,
> development of personnel, decisions close to the facts,
> flexibility—in short, all the qualities necessary for an
> organization to adapt to new conditions. From coordina-
> tion we get efficiencies and economies.[4]

This management model represented some of the first efforts to "empower" key managers and to recognize their need for some measure of autonomy.

But the paradoxical concept of *decentralized coordination* was not easy to apply or sustain. Thus, as with many companies, the balance at General Motors shifted more toward coordination and bureaucratic control. This accounts for GM's painfully slow reaction to changing consumer tastes and strong competition from foreign automobile manufacturers during the late 1970s. Foreign manufacturers were much quicker than GM (and Ford and Chrysler) to respond to the new consumer demand for smaller and more fuel efficient vehicles. Consequently, as it entered the 1980s, GM's sales and profits dropped sharply, leading to cutbacks in production and widespread layoffs. At the time, GM did not have an organizational structure that enhanced its customer feedback mechanisms or promoted flexibility and adaptability. In the parlance of the knowledge chain, GM had no permeability between its internal and external awareness.

In an effort to mitigate the ill effects of the typical bureaucracy and energize those structures, GM and a host of other corporate behemoths in the same boat developed new, more horizontal, organizational formats during the 1970s and 1980s.

THE MATRIX ORGANIZATION

Perhaps the most famous and widely adopted of these was the so-called matrix organization, which skillfully combined elements of central control and decentralization. For companies that steadfastly resisted fully decentralized control (for example, those organized according to geography or product line) or a pure team management approach, the matrix organization represented a viable and workable compromise (see figure below).

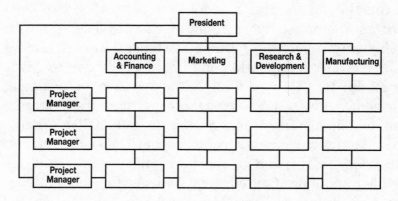

The matrix organization.

Many companies' biggest fears about a fully decentralized organization was the loss of coordination and potentially the diminution of the organization's coherence and unity of purpose. Would decentralization lead to chaos and confusion among employees? How would employees in a decentralized company identify who is responsible and accountable? Where would the locus of legitimate sources of authority reside?

But the hierarchy often instilled authority in an arbitrary and illusory fashion. Position endowed one with authority, without regard to whether the current skills and astuteness of the person in the position warranted it.

The matrix format was a simple mechanism to hedge management's bets. Even in Japan this became a popular structure, adopted by major corporations such as Asahi Glass Company, which hoped, in classic Japanese metaphor, that this format would allow the wind to blow through its static environment and regimented procedures.

Matrix structures were especially popular during the mid-1980s. For example, Pepsi-Cola had three autonomous operating divisions with an emphasis on channel focus: Pepsi USA, the Pepsi Bottling Group, and the Fountain Beverage Division.

Pepsi ultimately decided on a matrix-like structure with decentralized sales and marketing responsibilities located under each of the four regional presidents. Finance, human resources, and operations, by the way, remained centralized, though there were "dotted line" relationships to the regional presidents. Each hierarchical group within the matrix had its own marketing department, which often led to conflicts and redundancies.

The goal at Pepsi was to achieve better local coordination and cooperation while minimizing the risk of losing focus and functional excellence in sales and marketing. In this regard, the matrix organization has worked reasonably well for Pepsi and other corporations with similar objectives.[5]

Matrix organizations that emphasize decentralization and more localized control are indeed a step in the right direction. Their flattened structure promotes more local autonomy and should improve responsiveness and communication and expediting important decisions. But it is a far cry from achieving corporate instinct.

Controls can still be stifling and intrusive. In many matrix organizations, "the functional divisions retain most of the control, so the teams are set within a bureaucratic structure from which it is often difficult to break free."[6] As a consequence, their ability to innovate and respond creatively to environmental pressures is seriously compromised.

Matrix organizations that are most successful are driven by small teams that tackle projects expeditiously. The key is to develop the team approach with the right combination of technology and culture and make teams truly a part of the corporate fabric. Ironically, however, even the best and biggest matrices seem to inspire and reward people for circumnavigating the bureaucracy. In other words, those who advance fastest in these organizations are also those who ignore the limitations of the matrix and simply rally the resources needed to get the job done.

THE VIRTUAL ORGANIZATION

As computing technologies have come to pervade organizations, many observers have predicted a natural transition to the virtual organization, which they claim overcomes the shortcomings of the hierarchical bureaucracy and more horizontal structures such as the matrix organization.

Virtual organizations are supposed to dissolve functional boundaries and join disparate workers, both internal and external. In theory, they do this through technologies that allow almost all workers to share information immediately and simultaneously. Low-level workers (we use the term not disparagingly but in the metaphor of the traditional pyramid) can share information with top-level managers and engage in online discussions with middle managers and even executives.

We agree that, beyond any doubt, the technologies of a virtual organization have the potential to short-circuit even the most entrenched corporate hierarchies. Network technology effectively deflates corporate hierarchies by creating a stronger sense of empowerment, or at least awareness. It can also render the internal workings of the organization more intelligible to workers who will better appreciate and understand why things work the way they do—or, in many cases, why they don't work as they should.

There are numerous examples of companies that have done this on a limited basis with external constituents such as customers, distributors, and suppliers. For instance, U.K. drug manufacturer SmithKline Beecham PLC's global network collects product shipment and customer feedback data from other pharmaceutical companies, hospitals, and various health-care organizations. It culls this data looking for key trends in demand for a particular drug or for reports of side effects and quickly disseminates any relevant information back to its customers as a value-added service.[7]

Clearly, network technology has accelerated the development of viable "virtual" relationships, but networks do not *define* an organization's strategy or what it should be responding to. They merely give it the opportunity to respond faster. In fact, we believe strongly that the entire concept of a virtual organization is often driven more by technology zeal than good sense. Rather than cast organizations as *virtual* or *not virtual,* it makes more sense to think of *virtual relationships* in selected areas, which free the core organization to better express its own core competencies. But when you attempt to make every function virtual you lose the cohesion of the knowledge chain and, in our observations, actually slow it down.

Management guru Charles Handy has observed that, in the next century, the virtual corporation may simply be just a "box of contracts." This is not an appealing vision if the organization is to create the sort of permeability and necessary intimacy between the functions in each stage of the knowledge chain. Partnership and alliance may be greatly facilitated by virtual relationships, but these do not form an organization with shared purpose and instinct. Instead, virtuality brings together many organizations with separate and sometimes incongruous instincts.

The incorrect assumption is that a virtual organization can achieve its objectives by managing this cacophony of constantly changing, often unknown, resources. We have not seen this done on a broad basis across the many functions of an organization and have serious concerns about its effect on responsiveness.

This does not mean that virtual relationships cannot be formed with selected suppliers and functions, but these are often limited, highly structured, and not at all conducive to creating long-term corporate instinct. For example, Nike was a forerunner of the virtual corporation. From its inception in the mid-1970s, the company subcontracted manufacturing to low-cost Far East operations, though it was careful to exercise tight quality controls. It also used an independent sales force to sell its product. These moves enabled Nike to grow faster and to avoid high fixed costs. However, it astutely kept in-house the most critical functions that are its key success factors: research and development (i.e., design) and marketing. It was here, in these closely held functions, that the innovation and corporate instinct behind Nike's success was fostered. This is why we would argue that Nike is not a virtual corporation, but rather one that has established limited key virtual relationships with external parties. By outsourcing many other functions, Nike not only minimized its capital investment; it maximized its corporate agility by allowing its teams to focus on their competencies and react to the aspects of their business and market that were changing most quickly. While virtual relationships assist in establishing the periphery of an organization's supply chain, they do not provide the structure or the integrity for its knowledge chain.

Keep in mind that management continues to play a significant and measurable role, as does some form of structure. Our greatest concern with regard to the virtual organization is that it has connotations of a free-for-all structure that can be managed by technology networks— that attitude creates serious liabilities. It is one thing to manage the flow of information, yet another to manage the people to and from whom the information flows. Anne Brookings, author of *Intellectual Capital,* makes the inherent liability of this crystal clear in her description of the Barings Bank collapse:

> If people are an asset then effective people management is an asset too. Barings Bank is an example of an old company which failed due to lack of an appropriate management infrastructure.
>
> Their star trader in the Singapore office, Nick Leeson, was given responsibility for both trading on the floor of the stock exchange and resolving the position in the back office. This responsibility, which he allegedly abused, gave him the opportunity to misrepresent the company's position to his peers and superiors. The scam was perfected by staffing the back office with junior staff members who had neither the experience nor the seniority to identify any inconsistencies in the books and raise the alarm with Leeson's bosses.
>
> The absence of management control enabled £742 million, twice the value of the fixed assets of the bank, to be sent out to Singapore to fund Leeson's derivatives speculation. This was compounded by a questionable management decision to have the same person, Leeson, in charge of both the front and back offices. Coinciding with these failings was an individual who allegedly took advantage of the situation and single-handedly generated losses for Barings Bank of £827 million. Barings Bank, which had sprung from a trading company founded in 1762, with total assets of £5.9 billion in 1993, was sold on March 6, 1995, to the Dutch financial giant ING for £1.[8]

Although the staid Barings was far from a virtual organization, Leeson was set up to act as a free agent in the
context of a virtual relationship. And his actions illustrate
the supreme irony of virtual relationships—that they must
be managed with even greater structure and control than
is standard.

Corporate instinct, and more specifically internal awareness, is not simply a matter of making information available
to everyone within the organization but rather creating an
awareness of the relationships between the information,
processes, people, and relationships to the organization's
governing teams. Whether these teams exist in a hierarchy
or a flat peer-driven structure is irrelevant, as long as they
exist in a framework of checks and balances. These teams
must be intimately aware of and attached to the core mission of the organization.

Lastly, for certain key innovations, the reliance on the
virtual approach could be a fatal mistake. For example, a
Harvard Business Review article by Henry Chesbrough
and David Tecce differentiates between *autonomous* and
systemic innovations. Autonomous innovations can be
developed independently from other innovations, while
the benefits of systemic innovations "can be realized only
in conjunction with related, complementary innovations."[9]
The authors cite instant photography as an example of a
systemic innovation because Polaroid had to develop both
new film and new camera technologies. Another example
is the recent Advanced Photo System introduced by
Kodak, which requires everything from new cameras to
new processing equipment. The benefits of systemic innovations are that they tend to radically alter, and advance,
the existing state of the art. Autonomous innovations are
much more incremental in their effect. Take, for example,
the introduction of Kodak's new all-purpose Gold standard

film, which can be used in any camera built for standard 35mm photography.

The virtual corporation is a suitable mechanism for developing most autonomous innovations. But for systemic innovations the virtual paradigm is probably the wrong choice. The problem is that "systemic innovations require information sharing and coordinated adjustment *throughout an entire product system*."[10] But independent companies connected only by contracts cannot achieve a sufficient level of sharing and coordination. The complex information sharing required by systemic innovations will be more effectively achieved *within* a company than across company boundaries—unless the nature of those company boundaries changes profoundly.

After all, it requires a tremendous amount of knowledge to develop and commercialize systemic innovations. This knowledge comes from supplier and customer feedback, employee experiences with manufacturing processes, research and development findings, and so forth. The more complex and systemic these innovations tend to be, the more likely they will depend heavily on tacit knowledge and corporate instinct. Because this type of tacit knowledge is difficult to articulate and even more difficult to share across corporate boundaries, corporations that rely more heavily on implicit knowledge for certain innovation should eschew virtuality and opt for a more federated organization structure. Virtual organizations are also not conducive to the diffusion of corporate instinct, which flows much more slowly than explicit knowledge.

These many serious shortcomings suggest that virtuality is not the ideal organizational form. It is instead a component of an organization's structure—a means of establishing certain tightly controlled relationships with external parties.

THE PERPETUAL ENTERPRISE

Each of the organizational types we have described so far share one common feature—all are structurally focused or *spatial*. But achieving responsiveness, a key ingredient of corporate instinct, appears to lend itself to a chronology rather than a spatial structure.

Given the pace and substance of technological change, the abundance of organizational options made available by technology, and the need to ensure that organizational structure serves strategy, the optimal organizational structure for the twenty-first century is something we call the *perpetual enterprise*. Actually, because of its lack of a permanent structure, the perpetual enterprise is less of an alternative to the other structures we have described, and more a way in which to best enable any of these organizational forms.

A perpetual enterprise

- can adapt itself to its dynamic macroeconomic environment;
- is organized for continuous flexibility;
- is chameleon-like and can change radically from one project or function to the next;
- can simultaneously utilize hierarchical or vertical forms, and virtual relationships when necessary;
- relies on a federation of project-oriented teams rather than the more common departmental division of labor.

Warren Bennis was the first to dub this new species of organizational design an adhocracy, a term that captures the temporary nature of this structure.[11] But the perpetual enterprise is not a complete lack of structure. Instead, the perpetual enterprise incorporates aspects of all the structures we have discussed, including that of the virtual enterprise, when and where each is needed. Its principal strength is not merely the ability to connect workers outside of the traditional organization, as is the case with the virtual structure, but instead the capacity to utilize a multitude of organizational structures. It can be simultaneously virtual, horizontal, and vertical depending upon current market demands—and therein lies its power.

If you consider each of the previous forms of organization we have described, from hierarchy to virtual, it becomes apparent that each one is trying desperately to fight against the entropy that slowly dismantles organizations. But what if this entropy was a necessary phenomenon that could be channeled into an organization's mutation and evolution? In other words, it is only by dismantling the organization that we can continuously build it back up again in a form appropriate for tomorrow's market, economic, and cultural challenges. The key to dismantling and reconstructing an organization constantly is the ability to constantly maintain its knowledge chain—that is, its internal/external awareness/responsiveness.

This is why the essence of the perpetual enterprise is the quick and constant capture of codified knowledge—most especially corporate instinct—its implicit knowledge or "know-how," which is deeply embedded in the minds of its workers. This allows it to spin in a multitude of new innovations across many communities of practice, each of which may behave like an autonomous entity bound by the overall core competencies of the enterprise but not restricted by a single structure. The perpetual enterprise provides for the diffusion of *tacit knowledge* across all of these communities by capturing and disseminating it through the technologies discussed in Chapter 9. It also relies on these technologies to build its knowledge chain— that is, to heighten its awareness and encourage timely responsiveness to market shifts.

Interestingly, these perpetual enterprises are all knowledgebased and almost 100 percent capital intensive. Intellect is their product; it's all they sell. But we firmly believe that as other companies and industries become more dependent on intellectual aspects of their products and services, they'll have to follow suit.

MIT's Sloan School of Management has been involved for some years in a research initiative to identify the shape of organizations in the future. The project, called "Inventing the Organizations of the 21st Century," has developed a set of "coherent scenarios" for possible future organizations.[12] Sloan envisions that one dominant organizational form in the year 2015 will consist of autonomous groups of one to ten people performing nearly every task in the organization. These autonomous groups will be set up as independent contractors or small firms, coming together in temporary combination for various projects, and dissolving once the work is done.

It's important to understand that the "dissolving" of these groups when a project is done does not mean that the group's constituents "disappear." In the virtual organization one gets the sense of a group of mercenaries galvanized for a short-term effort. This is not what we are describing. Instead, we see a formidably rich organization of many skills and talents constantly being shuffled based on the opportunities at hand.

Authority in these autonomous groups is still evident, although not through commands. A small central company still has senior people who exercise their judgment over investment and marketing decisions. But groups also try wild-eyed ideas, some of which turn out to be very successful—and financially rewarding—for their participants. This structure is extremely well suited to rapid innovation and dynamically changing markets.

There is little doubt that the rigid and tight structure that has served to organize the corporation for the better part of this century is beginning to disaggregate in more and more corporations. However, full federation of the sort we are describing, or replacement of corporate structure with a corporate "antistructure," is only beginning. Some glimpses from our own market research for the Corporate IQ test provide ample evidence of this and the slow shift to perpetual structures. For example, while our research found that only 15 percent of the 350 organizations we surveyed say their organizations are still best characterized as a traditional tall hierarchy (and these responses, by the way, were concentrated among organizations that also indicated that they were in the declining stages of their market cycles), only 22 percent of the organizations we surveyed have federalized to some extent, structuring their organizations as integrated networks of teams.

The organizations we studied who described themselves as perpetual enterprises closely resembled an integrated network of business groups. These companies were characterized by a greatly reduced centralized control, and ranked decentralized decision making at double the average of all other respondents.

Another hallmark of organizations that characterize themselves as perpetual is a higher level of communication-based linkages between teams and people. In fact, these linkages enable the organization to communicate and coordinate strategy so that it is able to respond consistently. These linkages also serve as the basis for informal communities of practice, the key mechanism for transferring tacit knowledge. The implication of these factors, as backed up by our research, is that organizations with a perpetual structure are by far the most responsive and flexible.

One of the biggest risks of building the integrated networks that typify a perpetual organization is the inattention to building strong linkages between different parts of the organization. As a result, these companies may end up with pockets of networks, each unable to communicate effectively with other pockets. Coordination in such an environment is extremely difficult. These pockets are twice as likely to occur in organizations in decline, implying that they are the carcasses of failed organizational restructuring efforts that were not met with a corresponding change in organizational culture and processes.

Perpetual organizations are very closely correlated with decentralized decision making. Decentralized decision making has significant effects on all four aspects of an organization's instinct, especially its internal responsiveness. This is because it plays a significant role in learning and creating rapid-response teams. Nor does decentralized intelligence imply an inability to organize and coordinate. In fact, organizations that rely heavily on decentralized intelligence are three times more likely than average to rank highly for their vision.

FEDERATING: THE WAY TO EMBRACE A LOOSE, PERPETUAL STRUCTURE

How, then, can the perpetual organization be built—to take on a hierarchical structure, or a matrix structure, or a virtual structure, all in quick succession, or all simultaneously? The answer lies in federating the organization. The smaller the constituent particles (or groups) of which the organization is composed, the more flexible the structure of the whole organization.

The perpetual enterprise takes on the shape most fitting for the business environment at any particular time. Think of the business environment as a barrel. If the organization were composed of large, unwieldy groups, it would have difficulty adapting itself to the needs of the business environment, in the same way that large basketballs placed inside the barrel would not be able to fill the barrel without leaving large gaps. If the groups in the organization were smaller, they would be able to combine in much more flexible ways—like filling the barrel with marbles, which would leave much smaller gaps between their collective whole and the sides of the barrel.

Thinking of the perpetual enterprise as a large number of marbles is a useful analogy. The marbles, or work groups, form an organization only since they can combine to fill a container, analogous to responding to the business environment. But in order for this to work, the organization, currently one big unit, must be broken down into many separate yet closely collaborating units.

In place of departments or divisions, then, perpetual enterprises will *federate* into *work cells*. A work cell is a collection of people and roles. The people in work cells are extremely adaptable; the permeability between traditional functions within those cells allows for substantial flexibility in the workforce.

At 3M, for example, employees working as teams are empowered to take decisive actions on a daily basis. This empowerment comes with a commensurate measure of access to information that allows them to make informed decisions.[13] These teams are not only self-organizing but also self-directed. The ultimate form of this self-directed team is the work cell, or what we have also referred to as a *community of practice*, where the people take on roles based on competencies rather than titles and hierarchical stature.

By federating, the perpetual enterprise is the only structure that will survive change because it is the only one that never stops changing.

Federation enables corporate instinct to guide the perpetual organization to take on whatever form is most appropriate for current conditions. This is the only way in which it can assure its processes remain suitable to current demands. Workers are not only permitted, but expected, to organize their own work, and work becomes target oriented rather than rule based. Corporate snobbery gives way as strong emphasis is placed on a team approach. In place of institutionalized hierarchical positions and job descriptions, processes are accomplished by roles, or sets of skills, which are constantly changing.

Instead of expecting to plug into an ordered, predictable work structure, people learn to revel in their ability to get by in spite of constant change. A senior manager at a leading PC manufacturer told us, "We've gotten to the point where we expect change on a daily basis and are concerned if we're not changing that quickly." The perpetual organization is not a series of periodic restructuring exercises—it is inherently without structure.

Federalization is the only way in which decision making can truly be wrenched from the hands of management. Talk about worker empowerment and flattened hierarchies masks the fact that employees are still overridden when important decisions are to be made. In the Corporate IQ Test, more than half of the respondents claim that their companies value decentralized decision making. Yet two thirds claim that strategic decisions are made by a small coterie of executives in their companies.

A second advantage of federalization is diversity of exposure. As companies decoagulate, interaction grows with outside parties—customers, competitors, and partners—causing each area to adapt differently. This enhances the complexity of the organization, ultimately improving its ability to respond to unforeseen circumstances. An ability to convey this knowledge of diverse environments thus becomes critical.

Third, responsiveness is greatly enhanced. Teams can become more specialized, yet move quickly enough to mount useful attacks. Knowledge is not vested in the hands of management alone. Peter Drucker sees a new center for corporate knowledge: "Knowledge will be primarily at the bottom in operations with specialists who direct themselves. There will be few specialists in central management."[14] By federalizing, companies will have the chance to apply this knowledge without encumbering it with layers of bureaucracy and policy.

This also results in *disintermediation,* or the lack of middle layers of management control, internal, or external intermediaries. Large-scale and technological power enables outside parties to connect directly to the innovators' systems rather than go through intermediaries.[15] The benefit of disintermediation is an increased immediacy and a faster knowledge chain.

Brazilian firm Semco epitomizes this radical approach.[16] The manufacturer of marine and food-service equipment was forced to cut costs radically in 1990, when the Brazilian finance ministry instituted severe austerity measures and reduced the nation's money supply by 80 percent overnight. To survive the resulting crisis, management encouraged employees to form satellite enterprises that used company facilities, with Semco providing an initial contract to get the new ventures going and offering severance packages and training to assist employees in making the transition. The scheme allowed the parent company to cut payroll and inventory costs, and at the same time work with suppliers who knew Semco's business intimately.

A positive, though unexpected, side effect was the unleashing of entrepreneurial energy in the satellite firms. In 1990, the parent firm had 500 employees; four years later it had 200, with the satellites employing the same number and 50–60 more working part-time for both Semco and one of the satellites. But by 1994, the satellites were accounting for two-thirds of the new products Semco launched. The experiment created a more free-wheeling, experimental culture within the entire organization. Majority owner Ricardo Semler writes with pride that "no one in the company really knows how many people we employ." The lack of direction from management and the ad hoc, seemingly chaotic environment has only enhanced morale and performance in both the core company and the satellites.

IDENTIFYING WORK CELLS THAT CAN BE FEDERATED

If an organization is constantly changing its form or taking on a multitude of forms simultaneously, it must confront a serious challenge concerning the way in which work really gets done and mapping the relationships between people. An organization chart cannot accomplish this. A better way to map the work and the relationships is by mapping the communication between people. These communications reflect the communities and competencies of an organization. For example, imagine mapping the flow of e-mail to and from every individual in your organization. This would provide an immediate and up-to-the-minute view of the many forms the organization has taken, without regard to the individual's position, title, or function.

One way to visualize this is by mapping the organization as a circle. Along the perimeter write the titles or e-mail addresses of key managers, with lines criss-crossing to each other, noting the volume and frequency of their communication. This provides a much truer picture of work cells and communities of practice than an organization chart. It can also identify problems. For instance, consider an organization chart with the heads of marketing, production, and engineering reporting to the vice president of new products. Its map of e-mails shows that marketing is not talking to engineering—there are no lines between those two. But there are lots of lines between marketing and production, as well as between engineering and production. This signals that the VP of production is acting as an important liaison between engineering and marketing, in the absence of communication between marketing and engineering. The organization chart would not reveal this. And with today's proliferation of e-mail and networks, it is a relatively simple task (and not as invasive as it may sound, as the exercise monitors volume of communication, not the content).[17]

But e-mail is only one of many forms of digital communication that exist within an organization.

More complex communications in the form of documents such as memos, reports, and correspondence can be used to map communities of practice by casting what is called a *digital dragnet.* This intelligent knowledge agent can sniff out inferences of people's skills and competencies by intelligently reading through the digital products of their work, such as consulting reports developed by an analyst, résumés, or online presentations.

How you portray the results of these digital dragnets may be just as important as *what* you portray. For example, one product we have seen uses the metaphor of a color Doppler weather radar system—the sort you see on the nightly news. Different colors represent differing degrees of relevance or competency. For instance, a large red blob may indicate a pooling of competencies and the existence of a community of practice within an organization. This may sound simplistic, but the key to creating awareness lies in simplifying, not complicating, the organization's people, processes, and markets.

END NOTES

1. Schrage, Michael, "Get Real. One Metric Matters," *Forbes ASAP,* April 7, 1997, p. 56.

2. See H. Fayol, *General Principals of Management,* New York: Pitman, 1949, pp. 19–42.

3. Arthur, W. Brian, "Increasing Returns and the New World of Business," *Harvard Business Review,* July-August, 1996, p. 104.

4. Sloan, Alfred P., *My Years with General Motors,* New York: Doubleday, Inc., 1964, p. 177.

5. See "Pepsi-Cola US Beverages," (A) in Joseph Bower et all. *Business Policy,* Homewood, IL: Irwin, 1991, pp. 510–529.

6. Morgan, Gareth, *Images of Organization,* London: Sage Publications, 1997, p. 53.

7. Herwitt, Elizabeth, and Condon, Ron, "Why Get Connected," *ComputerWorld/Network World,* September 9, 1996, p. 23.

8. Brooking, Annie. *Intellectual Capital Core Asset for the Third Millennium Enterprise,* Boston: International Thompson Business Press, 1996, p. 8.

9. Chesbrough, Henry and Tecce, David, "When Is Virtual Virtuous? Organizing for Innovation," *Harvard Business Review,* January/February 1996, p. 67.

10. Ibid.

11. Bennis, Warren, *Changing Organizations,* New York: McGraw-Hill, 1966, p. 165.

12. Laubacher, R. J., Malone, T. W., and the MIT Scenario Working Group, "Two Scenarios for 21st Century Organizations: Shifting Networks of Small Firms or All-Encompassing 'Virtual Countries'?" Working Paper, Sloan School of Management, Massachusetts Institutes of Technology, January 1997.

13. Williams, Ron, "Self-Directed Work Teams: A Competitive Advantage," *Quality Digest*, November 1995, p. 50.

14. Drucker, P. F., "The Coming of the New Organization," *Harvard Business Review*, January/February 1988, pp. 45–53.

15. Quinn, James Brian, *Intelligent Enterprises*, New York: The Free Press, 1992, p. 26.

16. Semler, R., "Why My Former Employees Still Work for Me," *Harvard Business Review*, January/February 1995, pp. 64–74.

17. Webber, Alan M., "What's So New About the Economy?" *Harvard Business Review*, January/ February 1993, p. 7.

8

The Achilles' Heel of Corporate Instinct

I not only use all the brains that I have, but all that I can borrow.
Woodrow Wilson

Trying to balance the freedom of thought which characterizes corporate instinct with a need to ensure a clear and consistent strategic approach can fracture an unwary organization. The Achilles' heel of perpetual enterprises is their susceptibility to the twin diseases of anarchy and impotence—unavoidable fates for even the most intelligent organization which cannot coordinate and communicate.

While federation without coordination spells disaster, there are three provisos that can secure the perpetual enterprise by ensuring a concerted strategic thrust without resorting to rigid management domination. They are:

- Coordination through communication
- Metaskills
- Communities of Practice

Without these, the perpetual organization is uselessly uncoordinated. There are plenty of examples of companies that stripped away central hierarchy and control and failed miserably by losing the ability to create a shared awareness of the organization.

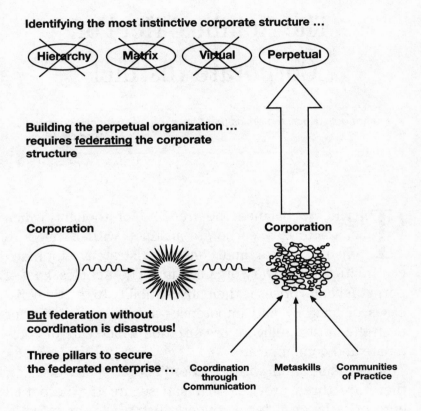

COORDINATION, NOT CONTROL

Without a rigid and dominant command center, a new form of coordination and strategic synchronization is required. But how can a single common intelligence emerge from a collection of apparently independent entities?

Decentralized organizations are not the first to exhibit this phenomenon. In fact, scientists have been studying what they call chaos theory for many years. Patterns of chaos can be seen frequently in nature and society—the weather system, traffic patterns, and the stock market are all familiar examples.

According to chaos theory as it applies to organizations, complex feedback systems—the cycles by which different parties or bodies influence one another's actions—cause increasing turmoil from changing customer requirements, competitive pressures, technological abilities, regulatory frameworks, and political and economic conditions.[1]

When a system is in a state of stability or equilibrium, it's very difficult for it to achieve a new state or behavior without a large infusion of energy. This is why organizations struggle so much to transform themselves. Put another way, the longer an organization avoids change, the harder it becomes to change. If equilibrium does not exist, though, companies tend to fragment and disintegrate. Success lies in a *dynamic-equilibrium—a state between stability and instability.*[2] Natural systems thrive on "persistent disequilibrium—continuously surfing on the edge, never stopping but never falling."[3] In this state, organizations are constantly challenged to become aware of their environment and to respond to it. In this state of near chaos, organizations gain maximum knowledge.

Dynamic equilibrium is so important because the ability to respond to a complex external environment requires maintaining the same level of complexity or diversity internally. The challenge, then, is to ensure that this diversity revolves around a common vision. Chaos theory proposes that synchronization emerges from freedom at play within some simple rules—namely, that organizational knowledge is shared and that a shared strategy is communicated through guidelines rather than hard-and-fast rules. Within these guidelines, the organization can retain the coordination of much more centralized organizations, yet have much greater flexibility to respond to new circumstances quickly and effectively. Thus, coordination through communication, rather than control, is the key to effective strategy.

The respondents to the Corporate IQ Test survey confirm this. The most instinctive organizations are heavily oriented around coordination of effort; however, they use means other than centralized control to achieve this. For example, the networked structure of federated organizations plays a prominent role in enabling strategic communication—in fact, this is the primary role of the organizational structure, according to such organizations. In addition, several other techniques emerge to ensure coordination and consistency in strategy. Cross-organizational communication and the use of a knowledgebase are both 50 percent more likely in these cases.

However, organizations with corporate instinct typically have much more flexible strategies to handle uncertain conditions. Even though the entire organization is involved in strategic decision making, they are 132 percent more likely to handle both long- and short-term strategy simultaneously. These companies are also three times more likely to rank the flexibility of their strategy highly.

Few organizations, however, can boast that they coordinate through communication, rather than control. Even though many organizations claim to have moved toward decentralization, and almost half of those we surveyed said their companies valued decentralized decision making, almost two-thirds of organizations relied on an individual or small group to formulate corporate strategy, as opposed to *only* 6 percent whose strategy is driven by the entire company.

A concrete example of coordination without control is the complex tangle of interconnecting networks forming the Internet, which has an element of haphazardness to it yet ensures direct and immediate communication among its many diverse users across the world. The precursor to the Internet was designed by the U.S. Defense Advanced Research Projects Agency (DARPA) in the late 1960s and early 1970s as a system to link its bases across the country. It is widely believed that the DARPA designers had a specific objective—to ensure that the network had no one single point of centralization, no single point of failure, that could be attacked by an enemy. The network had to be able to route information around any part of the network that might be attacked.

One of the most radical concepts of the Internet is its lack of centralized authority. While pockets of influence do exist, neither the U.S. government nor any other party is able to control this network, and yet it functions as a coordinated and productive entity. In terms of strategy, the Internet has a broad shared vision, and apart from some technical activities, the plan for the future contains little detail. However, the Internet is geared to respond to evolving needs. Every entity—in the case of the Internet these are Web servers—is autonomous, yet when the environment demands it, these servers orient themselves with a common purpose.

This self-organizing characteristic can be seen in the Internet's RFC (request for comments) process. Any user who identifies a need for some change or development of the Internet can draw up a document called an RFC. This document is mailed on bulletin boards around the world, and interested parties become involved in modifying and refining the development, until everyone is satisfied. The result becomes a new standard.

Not long ago a controversy arose about the supposed availability of pornography on the Internet. Spontaneously and independently, a number of working groups emerged, each with the aim of looking at the problem. The groups communicated with each other and standard control mechanisms evolved. Within weeks, solutions began to emerge: programs and protocols to permit adult control of access by children to such material. The time from the identification of the problem to its solution was breathtakingly fast. Other centralized, planned, and controlled organizations would have had to divert resources from elsewhere, where they would have to be "planned" to perform other activities, at great expense. These organizations would have followed the theme we mentioned at the start of this book, "Where there's smoke there's a committee."

Perhaps the master of coordination in place of control is Dee Hock, CEO of Visa International, the world's largest credit card processing organization with more than $1 trillion worth of sales. Visa International was born out of the credit card-issuing orgy of the 1970s, when banks were so eager to grab market share that they were issuing preapproved cards to anyone who could sign their name—and hemorrhaging red ink in the process. In desperation, member banks of the newly formed TransAmericard Inc. (later Visa International) appointed Dee Hock chairman, hoping that he would be able to impose discipline that the industry needed. But Hock had something different in mind.

Instead of a public or private corporation owned by stockholders, ownership took the form of nontransferable rights of participation by member financial institutions. Even more unusual, these member companies were fierce competitors in the card-issuing market. Nevertheless, these companies needed to coordinate on several key issues, such as setting standards, managing a common clearinghouse, and supporting a common branding platform.

Hock realized this inherent conflict, but instead of enforcing cooperation by restricting what members could do, he encouraged the companies to compete and innovate. Visa card issuers are free to issue, price, and service products completely autonomously. As a result of the diversity of approaches, best-of-breed products and processes are far more likely to emerge. That stimulates the entire industry. Hock says, "At the same time, in a narrow band of activity essential to the success of the whole, they engage in the most intense cooperation." This apparent conflict of competition and collaboration has enabled Visa to adapt to new markets, currencies, competitors, products, and consumers' needs.

Hock deliberately designed the organization to decentralize intelligence into autonomous units as far as possible. Yet the organization's strategy and cooperation are more coordinated than many centralized organizations. Visa has been called "a corporation whose product is coordination," and "the only company in the world owned by its franchisees." Hock calls it an "enabling organization." He attributes its success to the combination of free-market enterprise and multiparty democracy the organization embraces.

METASKILLS

The key competitive resource in many industries is knowledge; the need for "smart" organizations cannot be understated. But "smart" organizations are not just ones that know how to do their job. Corporate instinct looks beyond the discrete skills sets of the company toward the development of metaskills, which enable it to continuously evaluate, modify, and build skills. Crucial to this is a culture that continuously questions implicit assumptions and is prepared to make changes to even the most basic tenets of the organization when conditions demand it.

There are two methods by which an organization can try to accomplish this critical understanding: adaptive and generative learning. Adaptive learning is fairly straightforward: We identify a problem or gap between where we are and where we need to be, and set about solving the problem and closing the gap. Generative learning comes into play when we discover that the problem or gap requires new ways of perceiving and thinking. The process of identifying new problems, seeing new possibilities and changing the routes by which we adapt or cope will require rethinking and redesign.[4] Both are essential for any organization to survive. However, generative learning is especially useful when trying to cope with increased unpredictability of markets—or the inherent chaos we have been referring to.

Metaskills are the basic tool of generative learning. These help both the individual and the organization to manage their skills bases in times of uncertainty. They are typically not vocation or technology specific, but enable their carriers to adapt their skills and apply them to new sets of circumstances. In an instinctive company, where knowledge and experience requirements can change almost daily, it's not so much what you know, but what you can learn. As a result, metaskills are becoming as important as the base skills in many roles in the organization. Metaskills are aimed at ensuring three things:

SKILLS ADAPTABILITY

- the ability to learn quickly

- the ability to identify and question underlying assumptions and "unlearn" them if need be

- the ability to understand the business and view it from a holistic perspective

Autonomous Decision Making Aptitude

- the ability to repackage existing knowledge in new and novel ways (linked to imagination/creativity)

- personal initiative and leadership

- decisiveness in the face of incomplete information or imperfect conditions

An Emotional Aptitude for Change

- positive attitude toward ongoing change

- willingness to take risks

Metaskills are highly prevalent among the companies we surveyed. Two-thirds of respondents rank their learning competencies more highly than their knowledge of how they currently operate. These companies rank the serendipitous skunkworks approach to innovation through an experiment-fail-learn cycle twice as high as the average. Companies with metaskills are almost three times as likely to involve all people in the organization in the design of work processes. These factors are clear contributors to greater levels of flexibility—in fact, organizations with higher levels of metaskills rank twice as high as the average for internal awareness, and three times as high as average for responsiveness.

Organizations that take innovation seriously are 41 percent more likely than average to depend on serendipity for new business generation. Serendipity and an aggressive attitude toward risk taking are closely linked with responsiveness. Organizations that have a culture of experimenting with new ideas, and that accept failure in these initiatives as a positive learning and refining process, typically have a much higher track record of innovation, and find they learn faster and more broadly than organizations that learn through more traditional training programs. These imply a much more liberal attitude toward experimentation and innovation, as well as failure. These companies rank time to market more highly than development costs. Companies that define the primary source for product innovation as nonmanagement groups of individuals across the organization are 56 percent more likely to say that serendipity plays a significant role in their success.

In organizations where innovation is most valued, there is much less reliance on traditional sources, such as new product development groups or research facilities, for idea generation. Such organizations find that ideas are 34 percent more likely to come from nonmanagement individuals or groups across the organization, and from unusual sources such as accounting. This is because every individual and group is charged with developing multiple skills, experimenting, and exploring for innovation opportunities. Groups that do this are half as likely to be bogged down by bureaucracy, and are 45 percent more likely to take a good idea from the lowest ranks of the company seriously.

People may be predisposed to embrace or avoid these skills. But specific steps taken throughout the organization can encourage this form of learning:

- Champion willingness to learn. Many people fear learning something new, because it takes us into the unknown, where change is inevitable. On the other hand, as the world changes ever faster, learning is becoming necessary to survive and thrive. When the imperative becomes stronger than the fear, learning occurs.

- Don't worry about giving people a portable skill set that they can market elsewhere. Without such skills, they will not have the ability to work in the first place.

- Encourage people to learn on their own. Open doors to learning, but do not teach.

- Advance a vision of a better future that convinces people to make an effort to learn.

- Develop feedback mechanisms that enable people to learn from all activities.[5]

- Learn in groups, rather than individually.

- Provide role models and personal examples.

- Faster learning as a perpetual activity.

- Most important, create a climate in which the making of mistakes or errors is viewed as being in the interests of learning so that we come to embrace errors rather than avoid them.[6]

COMMUNITIES OF PRACTICE

Brain trusts are composed of individuals in your organization who have a vast wealth of experience and intelligence of specific organizational environments, and who are repositories for tacit corporate knowledge. These are the people who make a difference. The organization often becomes dependent on these people who know the answer to every question and can fix any situation. They are, in a sense, islands of instinct. And when they are lost, so is the vestige of corporate instinct they controlled.

But corporate instinct is not about islands—it's about a mainland of shared knowledge. Corporate instinct emphasizes autonomous leadership, both formal and informal, and continuously tries to contain the loss when organizational experts leave, by having insisted that the knowledge of these brain trusts become collective and continuously transformed into product.

Brain trusts must be identified and become sources of teaching. Their job should be not to perform the tasks they are so good at, but to teach others how to do them. By becoming team players, these brain trusts naturally impart many of their skills to others in the company.

As one CEO told us, "My job is to teach." If only every organizational hero felt the same way.

How then should information be communicated around the organization? In the absence of a strict command-and-control hierarchy, a communications infrastructure and knowledgebase must be put in place.

Knowledgebases can capture the explicit knowledge of individuals and teams and put it in document form. But tacit knowledge is not so easily captured. This may explain why only half of the companies we surveyed in the Corporate IQ Test have an explicit initiative under way to capture and disseminate organizational knowledge in the form of some sort of knowledgebase.[7]

However, the use of knowledgebases and central repositories of organizational knowledge is dependent on the kind of knowledge to be captured. While the true knowledge organizations we spoke with—those classifying all their workers as knowledge workers—are 27 percent more likely than average to make use of knowledgebases, it is interesting to note that knowledgebases are actually less common among organizations where tacit knowledge plays a prominent role. This corresponds with the relative absence of technological solutions in firms such as legal practices or doctors' offices, in all but the most technologically advanced cases. In these organizations, communities of practice and nontechnological forms of skills transfer are much more common. In fact, *structured* knowledgebases are used by only 2 percent of all companies for skills trans-feral. However, as technological advancement enhances the ability of technology to record and categorize more complex knowledge, we can expect knowledgebases to proliferate in these areas of industry very quickly.

Organizations making use of knowledgebases rank slight-ly higher in terms of their internal awareness, as well as their overall responsiveness. However, these rankings are not orders of magnitude above those organizations not using knowledgebases, which emphasizes that knowledge-base–related benefit is focused on explicit knowledge rather than on all organizational knowledge. Fully half of all organizations are biased toward tacit knowledge, which is difficult to capture and transfer, and which relies on extremely flexible and more personal interaction.

The most efficient way to transfer tacit knowledge throughout the organization is through the dialogue that takes place in communities of practice. These networks of people specializing in a particular competency or project have the greatest opportunity for knowledge transfer.

Communities of practice form and pull knowledge from individual members, rather than push information from the center.[8] Communities of practice emerge of their own accord: Three, four, twenty, maybe thirty people find themselves drawn to one another by a force that's both social and professional. They collaborate directly, use one another as sounding boards, teach each other. These com-munities are difficult to construct but are easy to destroy with rigid organizational structures. We believe that they are among the most important structures of any organiza-tion where innovation matters, but they almost inevitably undermine formal organizational structures.

In February 1997, American Airline pilots objected to changes in their pay structures.[9] Increased pressure from the corporation attracted the attention of the pilots' union, which called for a strike ballot. Though the ballot passed, many pilots and other employees were sure that strike action was not the right approach. However, their union overrode them and continued with its plans for a companywide strike.

This raised the ire of some members of the union. They decided to take matters into their own hands. Obtaining union members' e-mail addresses, these renegade union pilots sent union members details of their alternative propositions. They also set up a World Wide Web site on the company's intranet, providing answers to commonly asked questions and additional information to union members.

The barriers to autonomous use of these new technologies are almost nonexistent. In fact, they have become major technological enablers of the autonomy and communication called for by corporate instinct.

Communities of practice offer competitive advantage by quickly forging the human capital of the organization into knowledge.[10]

Communities of practice are more likely in organizations where the communication of tacit knowledge is common. Almost one half of all organizations we surveyed show signs of these communities, manifested through their informal methods of communication sharing experiences and knowledge. A quarter of all organizations frequently construct project-based teams from personnel across the organization, according to the value of the team member and the specific needs of the team.

Since communities of practice act as powerful media for exchanging tacit knowledge, general levels of awareness and responsiveness are raised. In fact, we found that in corporations where communities of practice play a role, responsiveness to the external environment is twice as high and internal awareness is 50 percent greater than the average for all organizations we surveyed.

The importance of communities of practice in building corporate instinct cannot be emphasized enough. Intellectual capital, the knowledge chain, even an organization's most brilliant innovators will remain largely untapped and dormant if communities of practice are not given ample opportunity to form.

Providing the foundation for building and the environment for fostering communities of practice is the most important reason for using the right technological tools for creating corporate instinct, and the subject of the next chapter.

END NOTES

1. Stacey, R., *The Chaos Frontier: Creative Strategic Control for Business,* Oxford, England: Butterworth-Heinemann, 1991.

2. Ibid.

3. Kelly, K., *Out Of Control: The Rise of Neo-Biological Civilization,* Addison Wesley, 1994, p. 470.

4. Schein, E. H., "Organizational and Managerial Culture as a Facilitator or Inhibitor of Organizational Learning," Working Paper, Sloan School of Management, Massachusetts Institute of Technology, May 19, 1994.

5. For more on feedback systems and "learning organizations" see, Senge, Peter M., *The Fifth Discipline,* New York: DoubleDay Currency, 1990.

6. Michael, D. N., *On Learning to Plan and Planning to Learn,* San Francisco: Jossey Bass, 1992.

7. Reimus, B., *Knowledge Sharing within Management Consulting Firms,* p. 1.

8. Manville, Brook, and Foote, Nathaniel, "Harvest Your Workers' Knowledge," *Datamation,* July 1996, p. 80.

9. Editorial. "The Deal-Breakers: How Renegade Pilots at American Airlines Upset the Union's Pact," *The Wall Street Journal,* February 10, 1997.

10. Stewart, T., "The Invisible Key To Success," *Fortune,* August 5, 1996.

9

Technology Tools
of Instinct

*The best metaphor for [technology] is as a kind of universal tool,
and tools over time do transform society.*
**Andy Grove,
Chairman and CEO, Intel**

In this chapter we will review technology tools that will enable and support corporate instinct. Some of these technologies have already been mentioned in previous chapters, but we consider them here in a more systematic fashion and in the context of an organization's overall information technology architecture. It is worthwhile to begin with a brief survey of how the current information technology environment has come about.

It is easiest to view the evolution of technology in three discrete but overlapping stages: the mainframe era, the distributed era (including client/server technology), and the new and emerging era of "ubiquitous" or network computing.[1]

In the first period, all data was centralized within a powerful mainframe accessed by dumb terminals or workstations. Many companies used their mainframes to automate basic clerical activities and to track financial and accounting data. According to James McKenney, they emphasized

"capturing and analyzing historical information and making it available to relevant managers. . .[and] to this end
they created active operations control systems to provide
timely information on planned versus actual and eventually exception reporting."[2] This architecture reinforced the
hierarchical and bureaucratic structure of many organizations, because information and data processing were cen-
trally managed and tightly controlled.

The distributed era began in the mid to late 1980s as
distributed database technology gave users the ability to
access data transparently across multiple computers
(including mainframes, minicomputers, and PCs) in a network. As powerful microcomputers and more sophisticated network technologies (such as local area networks)
emerged, the client/server model began to dominate many
corporate settings. Users with personal computers or
workstations (clients) linked together in a network could
communicate with each other and access data or programs located on a central server. Data was now more
widely and quickly available, and this facilitated more
decentralized approaches to decision making.

The emerging era of "network computing" represents a
truly *network-centric* approach. It differs from the
client/server model in several ways. Data can be transferred with greater speed and efficiency; also, software
will no longer need to be physically located on each
machine, but can be downloaded from a central server
(such as the Internet) when needed. Further, it is dominated by technologies such as the Internet, intranets (the
corporate equivalent of the Web), and groupware software, and by the easy exchange of data without the need
to worry about conversions or compatibility issues.

As network computing becomes more ubiquitous, how
do corporations develop an information technology infra-

structure or architecture that will help their organizations to become more keenly aware and responsive? An organization's information technology architecture involves several components: hardware platforms, communications platforms, information management software, and tools for information communication and dissemination.

Our chief concern is with the last three categories— tools that provide connectivity and portability, manage information, and facilitate its diffusion throughout the organization, unencumbered by cultural or technological obstacles. The ultimate purpose of these systems is the preservation and selective diffusion of an organization's broad knowledgebase, which is the foundation of corporate instinct. They help create the pervasive awareness that is typically present in instinctive enterprises. For example, Nonaka and Takeuchi cite Kao, Japan's leading housewares and chemical products company, as an illustration of how some Japanese companies promote organizational knowledge creation. A major business principle of Kao is "free access to information," and this is realized through a series of databases with detailed information on sales, marketing, production, and distribution. Anyone in the organization has full access to this database system at any time. Kao believes that this egalitarian approach to information sharing has enriched employee interactions, and this in turn has led to the generation of many creative ideas. In the framework of this book, it is clear that information technology systems in conjunction with the "free access" principle have provided the foundation to endow Kao with a good measure of corporate instinct.[3]

TOOLS FOR CREATING CORPORATE INSTINCT

It is far easier to manage and track explicit knowledge than knowledge that is implicit or tacit. Yet because the latter is so important, we must find a way to capture it electronically before it is lost or forgotten. Although some of this knowledge is bound to be elusive, it is possible to capture pieces of knowledge in specialized systems. In these cases a conscious effort must be made to convert tacit knowledge into explicit knowledge. This takes place in a dialogue between employees and often involves the use of metaphors and analogies to help conceptualize the unthematic. Consider the case of Nissan's "Primera" project, a so-called "global car" targeted primarily to European drivers. In preparation for production in England, Nissan sent many of the British engineers to Japan to assimilate accumulated tacit knowledge about Japanese manufacturing processes. This valuable know-how became thematized in carefully prepared manuals which could then be easily transported to online systems in order to further accelerate its diffusion.[4] Also, a portion of this tacit knowledge will emerge, as the basic gestalt, or structure, of pivotal operations that become digitized. In other words, if information systems can somehow make the organization transparent to its employees, if the organization can build the self-awareness we have been describing into its systems, then it can indirectly capture some of this embedded implicit knowledge in the process.

In our view, as one evaluates explicit knowledge, tacit knowledge that is so often difficult to articulate will begin to emerge. As users make connections and appreciate what is not articulated directly, the implicit will somehow become manifest. This is precisely what is meant by "informating" the organization, i.e., rendering information more visible and intelligible to an external observer. According to Shoshana Zuboff, who originally coined the term, "As the informating process unfolds, the organization is increasingly imbued with an electronic text that explicitly represents many forms of data which were once implicit, private, or minimally codified."[5]

But how can this be accomplished to help create corporate instinct? How can the organization be transformed into such a transparent and self-aware entity—what we have called a knowing enterprise? A number of technologies make this possible. They can be divided into six basic categories:

- networks
- enterprise-wide information systems
- knowledgebases
- workflow
- visualization
- process simulation

Networks

Networks essentially provide the grand infrastructure for exchanging and transferring information. They are unquestionably ushering in the ubiquitous era of computing. The network of networks is of course the Internet. This vast global network now links nearly one hundred million individuals and organizations throughout the world. The Internet provides *global connectivity* along with a platform for information exchange, enabling users to communicate efficiently and rapidly.

The World Wide Web, an application of the Internet, has greatly accelerated the use of this global network for commercial purposes. The Web was developed at the European Particle Physics Lab as a means of exchanging data about high-energy physics among physicists scattered throughout the world. This group developed a standard known as HTML or hypertext markup language that supports a procedure whereby "tags," or triggers, are attached to a word or phrase that links it to another document located anywhere on the Internet. That document can be in a multimedia format, including video, text, images, and even sound. Net browser software such as Netscape (based on the original Mosaic model) allows users to access all these formats on the Web effortlessly.

The Web has many uses for commercial enterprises. It is a rich source of customer data that can greatly enhance external awareness and responsiveness. For example, some companies, like L'eggs pantyhose, use the Web to increase their proximity to and intimacy with the end consumer. L'eggs incorporated a customer forum within its Web site where customers can provide instantaneous product feedback—external awareness. Many companies are using similar approaches to better appreciate customer preferences that can be immeasurably important for making product or marketing enhancements—external responsiveness. As one observer noted, "The corporate craze for customer service is launching a proliferation of Web-based systems that offer self-service to customers and customer information to companies."[6]

Many companies are also developing *intranets*—an internal network built on the same technology that comprises the World Wide Web, specifically HTML and HTTP (hypertext transfer protocol). Intranets may be run over private WANs (wide area networks) or the Internet.

By leveraging the Web, intranets can offer substantial cost savings over the use of traditional wide area networks. Rather than using dedicated lines, remote users simply access the intranet by way of Internet service providers, or ISPs. Clearly the intranet facilitates the development of an organization without boundaries sharing information and processes across its entire value chain of activities.[7]

Network computing technologies such as intranets integrate computers and communications and link organizations in ways that transcend the constraints of time and space. They greatly simplify and streamline direct communications with external groups such as customers and suppliers. For example, intranet-to-intranet communications might allow one company to order supplies from several linked suppliers and have those different supplies shipped all at once. In this way, companies can become more virtual and efficient by focusing on their core resources, those functions where they truly add value, and letting other organizations, integrated through networks, perform the remaining functions.

By more closely connecting all of their major constituencies, customers, suppliers, collaborators, and employees in remote locations, networks *transfer information* that is critical for the cultivation of corporate instinct. Thanks to networking, a company has instant access to information from sources inside and outside the organization. This more immediate and richer feedback creates a solid foundation for enhancing overall awareness and responsiveness.

ENTERPRISE-WIDE INFORMATION SYSTEMS

These systems are designed to provide a comprehensive overview of the dynamics of the business and the industry in which it competes. A *data warehouse,* for example, is essential for supporting decisions based on thorough empirical data. A data warehouse is a robust database or data-storage facility that contains information about products, distribution channels, customers, competitors, and suppliers. These broad categories might represent segments of the warehouse that provide a different view of the business. A data warehouse is usually designed to be quite comprehensive, but many focus on customer and product data. For example, Owens & Minor, a $3 billion distributor of medical supplies, uses its warehouse primarily to track background information about customers along with extensive purchase histories.

An efficient data warehouse, then, integrates collected information into a logical model of different subject areas and makes this information accessible across the enterprise. The goal is to provide an "enterprise-wide view of the business."[8]

Enterprise-wide management tools can also help to create the necessary connections between disparate parts of an organization and its knowledge chain. This is done by using an interconnected set of spreadsheet-like databases or tables that reflect the state of affairs in even the most dynamic businesses in as timely a manner as possible.

Colgate Palmolive, for instance, uses this approach to manage its complex inventory, but this is far more than a typical inventory management tool. The great benefit of this sort of system is its ability to perform immediate and simultaneous updates. For example, when a key ingredient is added to a Colgate product on the production floor, a worker updates the local table and this reverberates throughout Colgate's knowledgebase. It shows each linked unit (including the supplier of this material) that these ingredients have been used and that the shipment of the final product is that much closer to reality.

Colgate is also linking its network to those of its suppliers and customers in order to detect changes in demand instantaneously (instead of a month later after a summary sales report is generated). The effect is that Colgate knows intimately what, where, and how its customers are buying, and is able to immediately incorporate this knowledge into its supply chain.

If this system works as Colgate plans, it will allow the company to perfect its just-in-time inventory strategy: to target production more efficiently and keep its finished goods and raw material inventories to their barest minimum without jeopardizing sales.

The company is imbued with the organic electronic text we described earlier, which will undoubtedly reflect much of the knowledge that would have been considered tacit and buried away deep in its recesses.

This system is helping Colgate sharpen and refine its instinct, because it makes the company's awareness more acute and promotes almost immediate responsiveness to short-term demands. Meanwhile, the company's knowledge of sales trends and other data will help it to be far more responsive to long-run demands and industry changes.

Finally, companies seeking to leverage corporate instinct must be more creative in the types of information they collect and manage. This may lead to a whole new species of enterprise-wide systems. In their quest for getting the right information and turning that into valuable knowledge, companies must ask some of the following questions.

- What sort of information do we need in this organization?

- What are the likely sources of this information?

- When and how do we get it?

- When do we need it?

- Which members of the organization require access to this information?

Answering these questions will help companies develop a grand and comprehensive information strategy that will serve as a basis for developing their information systems.

Much of the information companies require for their knowledgebase is explicit. For example, most companies realize the they need copious market and production data which should be carefully integrated into their information systems. This might include comprehensive data about which products customers are purchasing in different regions of the country or information on product assembly and cost accounting.

However, in order to capture important sources of knowledge that are not so explicit, companies must begin to probe the level of personal and tacit knowledge among the organization's primary stakeholders, especially customers, suppliers, and employees. These might include employees' opinions and feelings about customer satisfaction issues, the need for improvement in certain processes, or hunches about the competition. In order to uncover and preserve this more ambiguous type of knowledge, organizations will need to develop some unconventional repositories of information. Thomas Davenport suggests that organizations develop "discussion databases" as part of an electronic memory system.[9] These databases could be a viable medium for capturing tacit knowledge even if this must sometimes be accomplished with the help of metaphors and analogies. The bottom line is that companies must be more creative and progressive as they construct the information systems that will help engender corporate instinct.

WORKFLOW

While the application of information technology to work design is not entirely new, its combination with self-organized process innovation is. Workflow, for example, is a set of computer-based methodologies and technologies that enable the analysis, compression, and automation of business activities.[10] It enables workers to visualize and orchestrate work activities for the first time. Workflow information systems allow workers to buy into the change process as never before, because they are able to understand it and control it.

Workflow tools achieve this by being

- self-service (users manage key elements of the processes themselves)

- process-centric (tools focus on the process as the basic entity to be managed)

- reflective (users are able to understand their relationship to the overall process)

Workflow tools capture process descriptions, perform statistical simulation and modeling of processes, and permit workers to explore "what-if" scenarios. In addition, the tools help define and monitor the metrics for continual process improvement.

How does this look in practice? Each worker in the organization is able to monitor from his or her desktop the business processes in which he or she is involved. This includes both the design of the processes and their current status, as managed by a corporate electronic repository. As the need arises for the processes to change, either as a result of a change in work requirements or because of new capabilities, the worker is able to make immediate adaptations to the process using the workflow tools.

These processes are defined in terms of *roles, rules,* and *routing instructions,* the fundamental building blocks for defining a process: *Roles* refers to the skill sets required to complete the process; *rules* are the specifications of the desired results; and *routing instructions* describe how the work is to flow. Thus, people can be reassigned to the process according to their skill sets and experiences. This technology-enabled approach greatly enhances process responsiveness and improves the organization's ability to innovate as people apply their knowledge of the process to changing business conditions. A questioning, searching culture develops as people throughout the organization are able to understand processes and change them.

VISUALIZATION

Change, in almost any scenario, requires not only a vision and a commitment to the ideal of change, but a set of enabling tools. These tools are not just the technologies used to implement new systems, but more importantly, the technologies used to help teams build visual models of existing and planned processes. Visualization allows for collaborative input and constructive analysis—by everyone involved in the process, not just the analysts and the developers. This concept is explored in more detail in Thomas Koulopoulos' *Smart Companies, Smart Tools.*

In their most basic form, these tools offer the ability to visualize a process in intimate detail. This goes beyond just describing or listing the steps of a process. A traditional approach to this, using a drawing or illustration package, is not enough, however. The tools must be capable of capturing certain parameters about the process that can be used for interpretation, analysis, and discussion. Ideally, a visualization both depicts the process and also helps to analyze it.

Visualization is also a basic element of systemic thinking, which provides the context often needed to understand the collection of events that make up a process.
Michael McGill and John Slocum, Jr., authors of *The
Smarter Organization: How to Build a Business that
Learns and Adapts to Marketplace Needs,* describe systemic thinking as "the ability to see connection between
event, issue, and data point—to think of the whole rather
than the parts."[11] It is this Mount Everest–scale view that
so often escapes the grasp of workers and managers, and
impedes process improvement.

To understand how these tools work, envision an electronic white board with the ability to spontaneously create
a visual rendering of your process as a team discusses the
steps and architecture of the process. As conflicting views
arise, the process depiction acts as a common storyboard
for individuals to agree or disagree with. If decision points
arise in a process, multiple nodes are created for each
branch, and when the process depiction is close to com-
pletion, the times associated with the tasks and information transfer are solicited from the same team. At any
point in time, everyone in the room is faced with a single
comprehensive view of the process. An immediately responsive corporate memory of the process has evolved,
which means no more flipping through several hundred
policies and procedures manuals to recall the specific flow
of a process; it is all there in front of you and every other
participant.

A facility of this type is a necessity for complex processes that have evolved over long periods of time, especially
in highly fragmented and specialized organizations. Don't
discount the value of a visualization tool until you have
actually used one. No amount of analysis can roll back the
clock to uncover the myriad decisions that created the

current process—visualization included. But a common understanding of how the process works will offer an objective baseline from which to challenge assumptions and create a shared vision of change.

Here are some of the basic components to look for in these tools.

- Drag-and-drop palette of icons representative of the steps in your process. These should be immediately recognizable by the users as depicting familiar events, people, and activities. Ideally, the palette should allow you to create your own icons so that you can reinforce the visual cues that already exist in your organization, or perhaps model the icons after you have chosen a workflow product metaphor.

- A desktop for diagramming complex processes with the icons and a variety of linkages, for example, whether the link between two steps in a process is electronic or paper.

- The ability to drill down and roll up the diagrams (this provides the visual equivalent of flying at a low altitude to see detail or a high altitude to view the overall scene) so that complex processes can be navigated and displayed easily. Having an electronic tool does not do much for you if you have to print out wall-sized diagrams each time you sit down and discuss the process flow.

- The ability to define parameters for each icon, link, and process. For instance, you may want to track pay rates, skill levels, and network IDs for individuals involved in a process.

- The ability to export captured parameters to a database, flat file, or workflow product. Once you have captured all of the relevant information about your process you may want to use a best-of-breed simulation tool to identify flaws in your process or restructure it.

A facility of this type is a necessity for complex processes that have evolved over long periods of time, especially in highly fragmented and specialized organizations. It provides a comprehensible, overall view, facilitates a common understanding of the situation, and provides a foundation for visualizing proposed changes to the process going forward that is easily understood by all the participants.

SIMULATION

Change, or more precisely the fear of change, represents the single greatest impediment to successfully creating a corporate instinct based on the collective and cumulative experience of an organization. Most often this fear of, or resistance to, change is a result of the unknown. "What will a process look like after change?" "What are the risks and the benefits?" And of course, "How much will it cost?" These questions may only come *after* the process has been changed.

Although simulation is not a panacea, it does provide an effective means for communicating the benefits of process improvement, determining the degree of risk involved with a given decision, and predicting the behavior of an organization, or at least a piece of it. Simulation offers answers to carefully constructed questions, such as "What is the likelihood that X will occur, within a week, given Y and Z?" What it cannot solve is open-ended problems without known parameters, such as "What is the best product to market?"

One of the most popular methods used for simulation is System Dynamics, developed at the Massachusetts Institute of Technology during the late-1960s by J. Forrester. The essence of this methodology is a holistic view of a system, or process, represented by multiple interconnected subprocesses. It is founded on the idea that any single process, such as insurance claim administration, cannot be accurately represented by a serial string of tasks, but only as a set of independently functioning processes such as hiring, training, promoting, claims processing, and so on. Visually, such a process (or set of processes) is represented by teeter-totter–like icons connected by long swooping arrows.

The obvious problems with any simulation will, of course, be the degree to which the human factors of a business process can be reflected in statistical measures. For instance, an author may know that it takes, on average, one hour to write one-thousand words of reasonably clean copy for an article. That rate may be sustainable over a two to three-hour period, but it is certainly not possible day in and day out for very long periods. There is some sort of productivity curve associated with the output of any human resource. In the case just noted, you could imagine a line that rises at a linear rate (increasing output as the author builds up creative energy), then begins to plateau (constant output as creativity and interest peaks) and finally declines (diminished returns as tedium and fatigue set in). It may also be a discrete function, meaning that it is not a smooth curve but rather one that works in fits and starts—not unusual for any creative or knowledgebased task. Once again we are forced to rely on heuristics that can only be gathered through real-world analysis of a *process*.

Unfortunately, nothing can replace the insights and information you obtain by getting deep into the trenches with end users. Ultimately, the true measure of a good analysis tool is the degree of intimacy it creates with the process and end users.

This is why it makes sense to use a tool that is able to capture existing metrics and create a graphical representation of the process. In addition, as the discovery process is often sporadic, rather than serial, the tool should allow a graphical model to be built piece-by-piece over time as users become more familiar with the nuances of their process. Perhaps most importantly, the tool should be free of product or methodology bias. In other words, the analytical tool should be a neutral ground for the free exchange of ideas between the information systems professional and the end user.

Much more could be said about the role of a technology infrastructure in support of corporate instinct, but that discussion is beyond the scope of this book. We have simply tried to illustrate how networks, databases, knowledge-bases, and other tools enable an organization to capture, extract, and leverage myriad sources of information and knowledge that help its workers to be more instinctive and innovative. There is no escaping the fact that corporate instinct requires the efficient and creative utilization of carefully designed knowledge-oriented systems.

END NOTES

1. McKenney, James, *Waves of Change,* Boston: Harvard Business School Press, 1995, pp. 18–32.

2. Ibid., p. 20.

3. Nonaka, Ikujiro, and Takeuchi, Hirotake, *The Knowledge-Creating Company*, New York: Oxford University Press, 1995, pp. 171–174.

4. Ibid.

5. Zuboff, Shoshana, "Informate the Enterprise: An Agenda for the Twenty-First Century," p. 230.

6. Hoard, Bruce, "Up Close and Personal," *Computerworld*, April 14, 1997, pp. 84–85.

7. Ibid.

8. "Planning for the Future: Data Warehousing," *Computerworld*, June 24, 1996, pp. DW2-7.

9. Davenport, Thomas, "Transforming the CIO," *Computerworld Leadership Series*, May 15, 1995, pp. 3–7.

10. Koulopoulos, Thomas M., *The Workflow Imperative*, New York: Van Nostrand Reinhold, 1994.

11. McGill, Michael, and Slocum, John W. Jr., *The Smarter Organization*, New York: John Wiley & Sons, 1994, p. 19.

PART THREE

Living with Corporate Instinct

*We all live under the same sky
but we don't all have the same horizon.*

Konrad Adenauer,
Federal Chancellor of the
Federal Republic of Germany, 1949–1963

10

The Economics
of Instinct

We need systematic work on the quality of knowledge and the productivity of knowledge—neither even defined so far. The performance capacity, if not the survival, of any organization in the knowledge society will come increasingly to depend on those two factors.

Peter Drucker

If knowledge has economic value, then the development of corporate instinct should have significant economic benefits for corporations. To test this, we must review some basic economic theory and discuss how information technology is reshaping some of the traditional assumptions of that theory.

THE CHANGING RULES OF ECONOMICS

Economists have debated for centuries about what makes countries wealthy. In his classic work on this topic, *The Wealth of Nations*, Adam Smith argued forcefully that wealth was equivalent to a steady increase in the output of goods and services enjoyed by society. This may seem like a banal and obvious thesis at the end of the twentieth century, but it was a ground-breaking insight in Smith's era when most people conceived of wealth as simply accumulations of precious metals like gold or silver.

According to Smith, a truly prosperous society exhibited a tendency to grow, primarily from a steady increase in productivity, which is simply an index measuring output (goods and services) relative to inputs (labor, equipment, and other resources) used to produce the output and usually expressed as a ratio Output/Input. Productivity in turn was most often facilitated by higher levels of investment in capital equipment, enabling laborers to increase productivity (i.e., achieve greater output with the same level of inputs). This increased productivity meant that society's supply of goods and services would continue its unabated growth.

Smith, of course, appreciated that capital was critical for the creation of wealth. He thought of capital merely as machines, equipment, and land, but other resources also qualify, such as information and knowledge.

Economist Robert Heilbroner provides one of the more insightful definitions of capital in this broader context:

Capital consists of anything that can enhance man's power to perform economically useful work. An unshaped stone is capital to the cave man who can use it as a hunting implement. A hoe is capital to a peasant; a road system is capital to the inhabitants of modern industrial society.

Knowledge is capital, too—indeed, perhaps the most precious part of society's stock of capital.[1]

Clearly, then, corporate instinct must surely be considered capital. In our view, it represents the most dynamic form of capital because it enhances the efficacy of other capital inputs. A company may make a huge investment in physical capital, but if it is not acutely aware and responsive it will not be able to utilize this investment effectively.

Paul Romer, a professor of economics at Stanford University, argues that knowledge and ideas constitute the primary engine of economic growth and that these ethereal assets matter much more than tangible resources such as land and equipment. Peter Drucker also makes this same observation, arguing that the basic economic resource "is and will be knowledge."[2]

For centuries, economic theory has grappled with the fundamental problem of how to allocate scarce resources. Anyone who sat through an introductory economics course remembers lectures about the trade-off every nation faced between "guns or butter." In a world of scarcity, tough resource-allocation decisions had to be made—countries could either eat well or have a strong military force, but they couldn't have both.

This problem was compounded by the perverse law of diminishing returns—the more one uses a resource such as land or machinery, the lower the incremental returns. Pessimistic nineteenth century economists like Malthus and David Ricardo predicted that scarcity combined with debilitating diminishing returns would threaten humanity's future survival.

Ricardo's dire predictions were wrong. His models failed to factor in the effects of information technology. The emergence of information technology has transformed knowledge into a vital asset and dramatically changed the rules of this game. In fact, each new development in computer technology that enhances storage, connectivity, and portability makes information or knowledge more mobile and accessible.

Unlike physical forms of capital, the resource of knowledge and ideas is inexhaustible and is not constrained by the law of diminishing returns. This reality demands that the rules of economic theory be revised and reformulated.

According to Romer's theory, "human beings ... possess

a nearly infinite capacity to reconfigure physical objects by creating new recipes for their use; by coming up with new ideas on how to increase, say, the power of a microprocessor, humans can boost productivity, spawn new opportunities for profit, and ultimately drive economic growth."[3]

To the extent that the law of diminishing returns has been defeated, growth has no limits—new ideas lead to new products and new uses for those products as knowledge feeds on itself in an endless cycle of new and improved goods and services.

A secondary benefit of increasing returns is falling costs. With new technology products like applications software, it becomes less and less expensive to produce each new unit. All of this clearly leads to an accelerating rate of economic growth. This is in stark contrast to the world depicted by Ricardo: "a gloomy state where the worker just barely subsisted, [and] the capitalist was cheated of his efforts."[4] Although there will always be some workers who "barely subsist," we strongly believe that number will diminish as the knowledge economy becomes more prevalent throughout the world, because information technology removes constraints on where, when, and how we work. Information technology also greatly expands the options for work design—this not only increases labor productivity but also stimulates the new ideas and concepts that drive the economy.

Technological advances allow companies to ferret out information that in prior eras was buried in an organization's dark recesses, and to share that information expeditiously. It allows organizations to streamline operations and expedite new product development.

If the key to economic growth is the diffusion of knowledge and ideas in their infinite manifestations and permutations, the key to corporate growth is the cultivation and proper preservation of intellectual capital. To be successful in the long run, companies must be consistently open to new ideas and innovative concepts.

In an era of infinite intellectual resources, supply is best measured by timeliness of delivery and not quantity. Innovation, in other words, counts far more than cost cutting, downsizing, or similar efficiencies. According to Romer, "It's the underlying rate of technological change that determines the growth rate."

To accomplish this, corporations must do a much better job of cultivating their corporate instinct. Corporate instinct—as internal and external awareness and responsiveness—leads to the timely creation of new ideas in response to marketplace opportunities. Those corporations with a well-developed sense of corporate instinct are constantly generating new product ideas, constantly innovating in response to changing market conditions.

Consider, for example, Nokia, the successful $4.6 billion Finnish company and its recent triumph in the mobile-phone market. Several years ago Nokia beat out market leader Motorola by introducing a digital phone with a five-line screen that allows users to send and receive e-mail and faxes. Nokia's goal is to keep churning out versatile hardware that works on cellular and satellite networks and to incorporate as much video and computing power as possible into its future models.

Nokia exemplifies the new rules of economics—it realizes that its most important form of capital is its ideas and knowledge, and it seeks to put those into practice as expeditiously and efficiently as possible. It's not physical capital or even human capital that counts the most in this game but "knowledge capital" and the ability to utilize it, over and over again.

CORPORATE INSTINCT AND DISCOVERY

If Romer is right, and the rules of economics have really undergone such a major transformation, there is a bright future ahead for most organizations that understand these new economics. Economics used to be the dismal science, but it is arguably becoming a science that pronounces hope and prosperity instead of the gloom and doom forecast by thinkers such as Malthus and Ricardo.

It seems to us that the main benefit of this new economic theory, where growth has few, if any, limits is the abundance of ideas and innovations awaiting to be discovered. If corporations want to reap the rewards of this new economy, their primary goal must be discovery and exploration. But how precisely does discovery of new ideas and innovative perspectives occur?

The discovery process begins with clues based on workers intuition, which feeds the imagination allowing the workers to "see" an old product in a new light, develop an idea for a new product, or product feature that will accommodate the needs and desires of its customers. This is a mysterious process, usually learned instinctively over time by example and practice.

Beyond any doubt, corporate instinct leads to a rapid discovery and implementation of new ideas and product concepts. If corporate instinct is unleashed, if knowledge management and decision making are truly decentralized, the end result will be fruitful explorations and timely discoveries that will lead to the perpetually increasing returns described by economists like Romer.

Global networks, intranets, and sophisticated knowledgebase software can play an important role in this process. They can augment corporate instinct and help to accelerate and inform the discovery process. Since major systematic innovations rely heavily on numerous clues and bits of tacit knowledge, the collaboration process can be stymied if this sort of information diffuses too slowly through an organization. But technology permits a far more rapid rate of diffusion.

The Ford Motor Company, for instance, has recently inaugurated "Ford 2000," which is designed to accelerate product development processes among its different divisions scattered throughout the world. In this system, "networks let designers expedite and refine design decisions before they are realized in clay, fiberglass, and steel."[5] Thus, a Ford engineer with a new concept for a light truck design can confer with colleagues in Europe about detailed topics such as "the spatial relationship between suspension and brake parts."[6] This allows the engineer to incorporate others' intuitive knowledge into his own design; his imagination for this new product gets a major boost from this sort of instantaneous and visual communication.

Information technology plays a major role in this new knowledge-based economy by helping workers and managers develop imaginative new ideas in collaboration with others who contribute their own insights and instincts to the endeavor. All of this encourages the creativity, collaborative imagination, and the multiple new product concepts that function as the engine of this new economy where knowledge and instinct reign supreme and where the old specter of diminishing returns, although not yet overcome, seems to be on its way out.

END NOTES

1. Heilbroner, Robert, *The Making of Economic Society*, Englewood Cliffs, NJ: Prentice-Hall, Inc., 1975, p. 86.

2. Drucker, Peter, *Post Capitalist Society,* Oxford, England: Butterworth Heinemann, 1993, p. 7.

3. Kelly, Kevin, "The Economics of Ideas," *Wired,* June 1996, p. 150.

4. Heilbroner, Robert, *The Worldly Philosophers,* New York: Simon & Schuster, 1969, p. 94.

5. Surgis, Oscar, "Behind the Wheel," *The Wall Street Journal,* November 18, 1996, p. R14.

6. Ibid.

11

Leadership in the Knowing Enterprise

And when we think we lead we are most led.
Lord Byron

Whether you lead one hundred thousand people, a small business, a team, or a start-up, one of the most pressing questions when it comes to corporate instinct is that of leadership style. Specifically, what primary leadership qualities enhance the creation of corporate instinct?

The demands of leadership have changed dramatically during the last fifty years. As the corporate environment has undergone upheaval and as traditional corporate structures have been overhauled, the role of the CEO has also undergone a significant transformation.

The command-and-control enterprise (critiqued in Chapter 7) regards leadership as the exercise of power and control. One strong-willed individual, a Henry Ford, for example, takes charge and dominates decision making in the organization.

But the dismantling of the hierarchy, the deflation of bloated bureaucracy, and the advent of individualism and free agency means that leaders can no longer emphasize such control along with blind subservience to corporate ideals and management by intimidation. CEOs must lead in different ways that take into account flatter structures, decentralized decision making, and the necessity for empowering and yielding more authority to the rank and file workers. Yet they must still foster harmony and commitment. CEOs in this new era must create instead of control. They must strive to create instinct in their firms.

LEADERSHIP STYLES—HOW CEOS LEAD

How then should CEOs lead in an aggressive, chaotic economic environment of global cooperative capitalism?[1] How can they best mobilize their organizations for the constant changes demanded by this volatile macroeconomic context? It should come as no surprise that the most important of these qualities, in our estimation, is the capacity for stimulating and promoting corporate instinct. But there is not one style by which to do this. Nor are the six styles we will discuss necessarily mutually exclusive. Each has its merits, time, and place. As we will see, nurturing a long-term set of attitudes that foster corporate instinct requires the ultimate test of strong leadership— the willingness to often step aside and allow the organization to take its own course.

THE MECHANIC

Some corporations need to be fixed. These ailing organizations usually require (at least initially) more hands-on attention than visionary, proactive leadership. When Louis Gerstner launched his massive turnaround of the beleaguered IBM Corporation with a proposal for $8.9 billion in cutbacks, he pointed out to a skeptical press, "The last thing IBM needs right now is a vision."[2] Instead, it needed a corporate mechanic, who could make hard decisions about where to cut and how to focus better in each division. Gerstner was well suited for this role given his background at McKinsey & Company, which specializes in helping companies through tough turnaround situations.

The mechanic must *execute* especially well. He or she is usually a "hands on" sort of manager who pays close attention to strategic details. The mechanic must implement whatever short-term strategic plans will help the organization overcome its inefficiencies and retrieve its lost competitive advantage. The mechanic's major challenges include determining what can be saved, generating a sense of urgency throughout the organization, and, in extreme situations, figuring out the basis for the organization's future viability. The philosophy here is usually a simple one: survival. The corporation has to return to profitability and improve its balance sheet before it can make real forward progress. At Wang Laboratories this was painfully obvious as Wang emerged from Chapter 11 in 1993 to redefine its viability. CEO Joe Tucci had one overriding mission: to demonstrate that Wang was viable. These are daunting tasks that require singular and committed leadership. In no way does being a mechanic diminish the strength or the credibility of a leader, but the close scrutiny of his or her actions by the market and by customers does limit options for radical thinking.

Even a good mechanic, of course, will exploit the organization's knowledge in deciding what to keep, what to eliminate, and how to fix what is broken. A corporation, however, cannot be repaired until its internal and external awareness are in sharper focus—this must be the priority for CEOs working to build a responsive corporate instinct. In short, corporate mechanics must quickly go beyond simple repair mode if they are to be effective leaders.

THE CUSTODIAN OF VALUES

Preserving the corporate value structure or the status quo can be quite effective in certain contexts, especially in stagnant, low-growth industries where there is little threat from substitute products or new technologies. Consider, for example, the Lincoln Electric Company and its legendary success in the stable electric arc–welding industry. Lincoln has dominated this industry almost from the day John Lincoln founded the manufacturer of electric motors and generators in 1895.

Various CEOs and presidents such as George Willis have devoted considerable attention to protecting and promoting Lincoln Electric's distinctive culture and value structure. Those values include guaranteed employment, promoting from within, bonuses based on performance, fanatical attention to details, and overall product quality.

At Procter & Gamble, CEO John Smale personified conservative, traditional values of loyalty, steadiness, and conformity. He also managed to keep the company in touch with its internal values and external marketplace changes. Procter & Gamble has sometimes had its problems in dealing with smaller and more agile competitors, but its overall success during Smale's tenure demonstrates that sustaining traditional rules and time-honored values is not necessarily a vice.

In other contexts that require radical change, clinging to old practices and traditional value systems can undermine a corporation's viability. Bethlehem Steel's leaders throughout the 1980s chose to ignore cheap imports that were flooding the steel market along with more efficient continuous-casting technologies that had been developed abroad. They clung to their traditional philosophies of management and a pretty basic ideology: inflate prices, ignore marketing, and pass higher costs on to customers. As the structure of the steel industry dramatically changed, Bethlehem rapidly lost ground to aluminum companies such as Reynolds. Bethlehem's leaders should have been trying to cultivate agility and innovation instead of futilely attempting to preserve the status quo and an antiquated value system.

THE VISIONARY/INNOVATOR

Most organizations cannot thrive for long without bold ideas and broad strategic vision. There are many examples of such visionaries and innovative thinkers, including Phil Knight of Nike and Bill Gates of Microsoft. Phil Knight's simple but powerful vision for "running shoes," which few others could see in the 1970s, underlies Nike's extraordinary success. Visionary leaders can sense opportunity where others see only constraints and obstacles. They often spawn new product categories and sometimes new industries.

The visionary/innovator adopts an active and energetic style of leadership. These CEOs shape ideas and directions. They are usually not afraid to take big risks to see their innovations through. As Phil Knight observed in an interview, "Our philosophy is the same throughout the business: take a chance and learn from it."[3] For example, in the early '80s Nike made a risky foray into the casual shoe market with disastrous results. But it learned to develop products with a much better external awareness of the market. The role of CEOs like Knight is to keep alive this vital culture of continuous innovation and proactive forward thinking, even though there may be failure along the way.

THE CHANGE AGENT (OR REVOLUTIONARY)

Some CEOs believe that their primary objective is to pro-
voke ongoing change and renewal in their organization.
They are mavericks and gadflies who constantly try to
prod others into decisive actions. These CEOs seek innovative ways to create an environment of constant renova-
tion and *re-creation* of old processes in response to
changes in their various markets.

Craig Weatherup, president of PepsiCo's soft drink division, sought to create a sense of urgency even when things
were going well. He wanted Pepsi to abandon its "business
as usual approach" and to think in more forward-looking
and creative ways. To instill a sustained crisis atmosphere,
Weatherup called numerous off-site meetings of key managers and demanded that they work out a plan to move
from 10 percent to 15 percent annual growth: "There's a
freight train out there and it's called 15 percent earnings
growth. We're standing on the track, and we'd better figure
out something or it will run us right over."[4] Pepsi has struggled to realize this ambitious earnings growth due to
extended factors such as the emergence of "new age" beverages and private labels. Nonetheless, this sort of crisis
mentality forces an organization to be proactive and to
keep changing even in the midst of success and prosperity.

Jack Welch, General Electric CEO, is another example
of this leadership approach. When Welch first joined GE in
1981 he quickly became an architect of change to re-
energize the then moribund corporation. He emphasized
the need to simplify procedures, delayer, and revise
entrenched staff roles so that workers could become more
responsive to market challenges.

He has also continued to fight against complacency at
GE. Welch has worked tirelessly to get his managers to be
drivers of change rather than planners or guardians of the

status quo. His famous work-out sessions get top and middle managers to listen to their workers, customers, and suppliers in a controlled environment. According to Welch, "Work-out will expose leaders to the vibrations of their business—opinions, feelings, emotions, resentments, not abstract theories of organization and management."[5] As this important feedback is assimilated, managers at GE will be forced to keep changing and innovating as they implement the best ideas that emerge from these invaluable sessions.

THE KNOWLEDGE CHAMPION

Some CEOs passionately devote themselves to the task of increasing the organization's knowledge. Their primary function is "to select, cultivate, and spread competitive expertise up, down, and across the business units of the organization."[6] Cultivating instincts and tacit knowledge is just as vital as developing explicit knowledge and skills.

Robert Cizik, CEO of Cooper Industries since 1975, clearly exemplifies this approach. Cooper is a holding company involved in three major businesses: electrical and electronic, commercial and industrial (for example, hand tools and the automotive aftermarket), and compression drilling and energy equipment; and well known for its extraordinary manufacturing expertise. When it acquires a new company, it adds value by restructuring and by helping that company to upgrade its manufacturing skills and process technologies.

To make sure the whole organization is focused on preserving and enhancing this expertise in manufacturing techniques, processes, and technologies, Cizik established a culture that recognizes and rewards those who demonstrate proficiency in state-of-the-art manufacturing skills.

The epitome of this expertise is found in the company's elite manufacturing services group. Whenever Cooper makes a new acquisition, experts from this group share their extensive manufacturing know-how. This might include new production methods, equipment, and the latest manufacturing technologies. This assimilation process, often accompanied by some restructuring, has become known as "Cooperization."

THE CULTIVATOR OF INSTINCT

This role incorporates some of the previous two approaches: the change agent and the knowledge champion. Because instinct involves awareness and responsiveness, the cultivation of corporate instinct inexorably leads to change. Therefore, the CEO who assumes this role will also be functioning (at least indirectly) as a change agent.

An instinct cultivator will build knowledge/expertise and self-awareness in the organization (internal awareness), develop an ability to understand the market's changing demands (external awareness), promote necessary change within the organization to meet those demands (internal responsiveness), and develop the organization's ability to react and adjust to changing market circumstances (external responsiveness). In other words, instinct cultivators help the organization acquire the abilities inherent in the four quadrants of the knowledge chain.

THE BEST LEADERSHIP QUALITIES

To some extent, the best leaders must support and advocate the corporation's values, develop relevant knowledgebases, cultivate instinctual knowledge, and never lose sight of the need for innovation and change. Leadership qualities of corporate executives in today's competitive era should manifest the capacity to create

- shared vision and ideals
- commitment and harmony (external and internal)
- corporate instinct

We observed above that the "corporate mechanic" approach to leadership might not require an immediate vision as the company seeks to recover from its various maladies. But at some point the chief executives of such organizations must remove their hats as mechanics and begin to articulate a clear-cut vision or blueprint for the future. No corporation can survive for long without some sort of strategic focus and shared ideals.

This vision must be grounded in the corporation's key resources (or core competencies), including the human and physical assets, skills, and capabilities of the corporation. Every company must be aware of its core resources that will become the basis of its strategic direction. Furthermore, its CEO must make sure that his/her corporation exploits those resources as efficiently as possible in the pursuit of corporate objectives.

The second trait or "virtue" of leadership involves exercising power to secure *commitment* to the organization's vision and goals. Leaders like George Willis of Lincoln Electric realize they must use their power carefully to ensure that diverse members of the organization embrace and adhere to the company's ideals and values. This endows the corporation with a unity of purpose and cohesiveness.

Although organizations could and should tolerate some dissonance, there must be general *internal harmony* if employees are to cooperate for the sake of the common good. In decentralized decision making environments, this also amounts to *empowering* one's employees. In this way they will be more self-motivated and will more easily blend into the corporation's "harmony" without the need for coercive control. The challenge of leadership is to foster *external harmony* between the corporation's vision and resources and marketplace realities, including the continually transforming macroeconomic environment.

The third quality of leadership is the ability to develop *anticipatory intuition:* the awareness and responsiveness that we call corporate instinct. Leaders must create "learning organizations" where workers simultaneously acquire and produce knowledge.[7] To some extent, then, every CEO must be a *knowledge champion,* like Cizik, an innovator like Knight, and a change agent, like Welch, keeping the organization alert and agile so that it can adapt to changing circumstances. All of this is actually subsumed in corporate instinct as *awareness and responsiveness.*

These three traits or virtues of leadership are closely interrelated. Vision, commitment (or harmony), and instinct neatly fit together and reinforce each other. For example, one cannot develop adequate corporate vision and galvanizing ideals, the basis of the company's goals and plans, without acute internal and external awareness. Internal awareness helps firms to be appropriately "self-aware," or fully cognizant of their resources and strengths, while external awareness can help sharpen a corporate vision and enable an astute corporate leader to refine and revise that vision in the light of new opportunities or potential menaces.

Likewise, awareness and responsiveness (i.e., instinct) bolster the internal harmony that is so vital for success.

Instinct helps empowered rank-and-file workers to work in transforming and productive ways; this keeps workers satisfied, builds commitment, and contributes to the realization of key corporate objectives. Instinct also helps identify incongruities between vision and its implementation or between vision and market realities that militate against external harmony. In addition, by empowering workers, CEOs can take advantage of the richness and diversity of instinctive knowledge perspectives that can be found throughout the workforce, unleashed for the sake of achieving greater productivity and efficiency.

THE CORPORATE EXECUTIVE AS CULTIVATOR OF CORPORATE INSTINCT

The following case studies illustrate the actions of key executives who have created strong, positive instincts that pervade their respective organizations.

MARKS & SPENCER, LTD.

Marks & Spencer, Ltd., founded in 1884 by Michael Marks, is the United Kingdom's most profitable retailer. In 1995 its profits approached £1 million on sales of over £7 billion. Its stores, scattered throughout the United Kingdom and Europe, sell a selection of high quality clothing, footwear, housewares, and fancy food items under the St. Michael brand name. The company's philosophy is to charge moderate prices, provide good value for customer's money, and to emphasize a high level of service to its broad customer base.

Marks & Spencer prides itself on its close relationship with employees and suppliers. Employees enjoy numerous amenities (such as in-store doctors), generous benefits, and higher than average salaries for the retail industry.

This encourages commitment and loyalty to the organization. Marks & Spencer often helps suppliers pick out the raw material used in its finished products and freely shares its sophisticated knowledge and expertise in clothing, fabric, and so forth. It also stresses loyalty and responsiveness in these relationships and rewards carefully chosen suppliers with a steady stream of orders.

These and many other factors account for this retailer's consistent profitability and sales growth, but what stands out about this company is the tacit know-how executives have built up over the years. Its distinguished CEOs, such as Lord Marks and Lord Raynor, taught the organization how to get an instinctive feeling for the business by going beyond the examination of codified data such as sales reports or profit numbers. Lord Sieff, the store's merchandising manager in the 1950s under Lord Marks, recalls:

> Both the executives and the merchandisers ... should probe into the goods in the stores with seeing eyes and a critical mind. The department supervisor and the salesperson are the best sources of information. To depend on statistics is to asphyxiate the dynamic spirit of the business.[8]

The company's consistent emphasis on probing and "management by walking around" helped embed tacit knowledge of the retail business, a special instinctive know-how. Senior managers would walk around stores asking questions, examining merchandise, tasting the food, and talking to customers. Executive judgments and decisions were based on the knowledge gained by this constant probing, on impressions and on "sensible approximation."[9] This knowledge, though dispersed throughout the company, is usually not transcribed anywhere. Moreover, the knowledge of each manager is a limited piece of the inter-connected, communal knowledge of many M&S employ-ees. There is a "Web-like" character to this knowledge. What is significant is not the isolated insight or partial per-spective of one individual, but the whole interconnected system. This knowledge is unspecifiable, yet it is an invalu-able and inimitable resource.

Because the corporate instinct or know-how is truly pervasive and ingrained (in the most positive sense of that term), it would be quite difficult for competitors to repli-cate in their organizations. It has allowed Marks & Spencer to deal effectively with certain environmental changes and customer demands. Over the years, it has enabled them, for instance, to keep store designs and distribution sys-tems up-to-date, make product changes, keep up with fashions, and above all to stay focused on the needs, desires, and changing tastes of its loyal customer base.

Of course, this resource could be even more enduring if some of this tacit knowledge could be captured more for-mally. This would require a conversion to more thematic knowledge which, as observed in Chapter 9, takes place through dialogue and frequent interactions among store executives. Some of this could undoubtedly then be cap-tured and disseminated through groupware or the more unorthodox type of "discussion databases" also intro-duced in Chapter 9. This would enable M&S to more sys-tematically transfer and preserve this knowledge in some fashion, which might be quite important if Marks & Spencer were to experience an unlikely bout of manage-ment turnover or unexpected succession. In order to do a better job of creating instinct the company's current CEO, Sir Richard Greenbury, would be wise to employ these information technology systems more aggressively in order to capture and share internally this organization's wonderful know-how. These systems must begin to be as much at the heart of Marks & Spencer as its enlightened personnel resources.

KRAFT GENERAL FOODS

Michael Miles is recognized as one of the most skilled and successful chief executive officers in the food industry. He developed a reputation at Kraft for his superior consumer marketing skills and leadership ability and led the company to many years of higher sales and record profits by adroitly introducing new products, such as Philly Light cream cheese, and repositioning old ones, such as Velveeta, which was successfully positioned as a cooking cheese after its sales began to decline.

Shortly after Philip Morris purchased General Foods, it acquired Kraft and merged Kraft with General Foods in 1989. Kraft General Foods, or KGF, became the world's second largest food company. Analysts agreed that Kraft contributed far more to this relationship than General Foods, which had grown stale and complacent. They also suggested that instead of buying Kraft, Philip Morris might have been better off just trying to hire Michael Miles to shake up its General Foods division.[10]

But instead Philip Morris purchased the whole company, and Michael Miles became the first chief executive and chairman of Kraft General Foods. Philip Morris, itself an expert in consumer marketing, shrewdly realized that it needed all of Kraft, not just Miles. Like the executives at Marks and Spencer, Miles had created corporate instinct, a certain know-how about consumer food products, a tacit knowledge that was embedded in the structure and consciousness of Kraft and in relationships within and outside the firm. Like the retail skills of Marks & Spencer, this knowledge too was implicitly grasped, difficult to express, and formed an interconnected whole.

Miles explicitly sought to create an "action culture" where marketing managers could sense shifting consumer tastes and act accordingly. In the process, Kraft developed a capacity for extending product lines and reviving old brands with fresh marketing approaches. But its marketing acumen went well beyond the mind of Miles—thanks to his leadership it became infused and woven into the fabric of the whole Kraft organization.

The hope, of course, was that the merger would boost General Foods' consumer marketing skills and improve its ability to launch product-line extensions. In an interview with *The Wall Street Journal*, Miles conceded, however, that this would be a tremendous challenge: "We have to make sure this $24 billion thing doesn't start behaving like a dinosaur but continues to be an action-oriented and creative entity."[11] Miles clearly recognized the difficulty of creating the sort of corporate instinct, the awareness and responsiveness that he labeled an "action culture," at such a large organization as Kraft General Food. In some respects his apprehensions were well founded, since Kraft General Food has never quite lived up to the expectations of Philip Morris or Wall Street. This was due in part to Miles' retirement in 1994, and Kraft General Food's tardiness in coordinating the shared resources of Kraft and General Foods, such as, distribution channels.

In both of these cases, we see how certain executives have assumed the responsibility to create an action-oriented culture predicated on instinct or *anticipatory intuition*, and embedded in almost imperceptible ways within the recesses of the organization.

A large part of the leadership challenge is to create instinct in such a way that it can be more easily transferable within the confines of the organization but remain obscure to unaffiliated or competitor firms. As we have demonstrated, information technology (such as workflow and visualization techniques) can definitely facilitate the former challenge since it can help to expose tacit knowledge and make the organization more transparent, but it cannot help with the latter one. Once knowledge becomes explicit and codified, it becomes more vulnerable, and can only be protected by intellectual property laws such as those that protect trade secrets. However, even if an organization were to steal this sort of intellectual property, it would likely have as much trouble as General Foods had trying to diffuse it into another organization that, like General Foods, didn't have the awareness or responsiveness to turn it into corporate instinct.

In these organizations where all workers are empowered to rely on their instincts, tacit knowledge, and knowhow, they play a role in leading the organization. They help it adapt swiftly and move forward in the right direction. In the knowledge enterprise, leadership is distributed and delegated to those on the front lines, to workers who are in closest proximity to customers, suppliers, and other key constituencies. Savvy CEOs know that they neglect these "voices of leadership" at their peril.

Thus, leaders who succeed in creating corporate instinct ease the burdens of leadership. True leadership in the knowing enterprise calls for the shrinking of the CEO's ego, since his or her intellect, imagination, and instinct will no longer be at center stage. Instead, the center and heart of the company will feature a collective instinctual wisdom, the interconnected knowledge and imagination of its workforce, along with the information technology systems that help to preserve, transfer, and manage these invaluable assets.

END NOTES

1. This term was by Alfred Chandler in his book, *Scale and Scope: The Dynamics of Industrial Capitalism*, Cambridge, MA: Harvard University Press, 1990.

2. Miller, Michael, "Gerstner's Nonvision for IBM Raises a Management Issue," *The Wall Street Journal*, July 29, 1993, p. B1.

3. Willigan, Geraldine, "High Performance Marketing: An Interview with Nike's Phil Knight," *Harvard Business Review*, July/August, 1992, p. 99.

4. Dumaine, Briane, "Times Are Good? Create a Crisis," *Fortune*, June 28, 1993, pp. 123–127.

5. Tichy, Noel, and Charan, Ram, "Speed, Simplicity, Self-Confidence: An Interview with Jack Welch," *Harvard Business Review*, September/October 1989, p. 118.

6. Farkas, Charles, and Wetlaufer, Suzy, "The Way Chief Executive Officers Lead," *Harvard Business Review*, May/June 1996, p. 117.

7. Torbart, William, *Sources of Excellence*, Cambridge, MA: Edgelwork Press, 1993, p. 16.

8. Quoted in Collis, David, and Montgomery, Cynthia, *Corporate Strategy: Resources and the Scope of the Firm*, New York: IRWIN, 1997, p. 264.

9. Ibid.

10. See David J. Collis' *Harvard Business School Case Study*, "Kraft General Foods: The Merger (A), Boston: Harvard Business School Press, 1991.

11. Freedman, Alix, "Miles Gets Top Post at Kraft General Foods," *The Wall Street Journal*, September 28, 1989, p. A8.

12

The Imperative to Create Instinct

There is nothing permanent except change.

Heraclitus

T he pre-Socratic philosopher Heraclitus, from the great city of Ephesus, may have lived 2,500 years ago, but he clearly understood the fundamental insight of doing business on the brink of our new millennium: the only permanent reality is change itself. Heraclitus saw a world of perpetual flux, tensions, and conflicting realities, where stability is only an illusion. It is a powerful insight that holds special meaning and relevance for the information age.

Heraclitus, we surmise, could never have foreseen the pace of change that corporations must deal with today, such as advances in the technologies of communication and transportation, that have facilitated the development of global commitments. Similarly, information technology has greatly expedited continuous product and service innovations, and led to an explosion of available knowledge and information throughout the world. It is difficult for even the most well-intentioned firms to keep up. As

Walter Wriston, Citicorp's former chairman, observed, "The entire globe is now tied together in a single electronic market moving at the speed of light."[1]

This book has been about the need for organizations to react instinctively to the constantly shifting forces in this global economic environment that is "moving at the speed of light." It has provided a prescription for creating a corporate instinct that enables superior adaptability and responsiveness.

Change and conflict cannot be overcome. The trick is to be as agile and flexible as possible. We have offered a comprehensive road map for achieving this sometimes elusive goal of adaptability.

We have also tried to compel the reader to reconceive the rules and boundaries of the business game in this new era of global cooperative capitalism. Hierarchy and fiefdoms must give way to decentralized structures and autonomous workers; collaboration must replace insular atomic units or independent silos of specialized workers.

Yet the most compelling reason to adopt instinct is not found in the pages of this book but in the corporate graveyard that bears testimonial to the failed efforts of organizations that lacked instinct, that were unable to adapt even as they saw clearly the world around them change.

Sears, Roebuck & Company, an American icon, has been surprisingly flatfooted in recent years in its response to changing consumer needs and tastes along with competitive threats, most notably from the likes of Wal-Mart.

Sears *has* successfully transformed itself several times in the past century, most notably in the late 1950s and 1960s as it shifted the location of many of its stores to suburban shopping malls and developed product lines to suit the tastes and needs of its predominantly middle-class customers. But its latest transformation was a colossal failure.

In response to slowing retail sales and low profits, Sears pursued an aggressive diversification strategy. It purchased a 50 percent stake in Prodigy, the online network service company, and invested heavily in the Discover Card. Sears also became a major player in the burgeoning service business, with an especially strong commitment to financial services. It purchased the real estate brokerage firm, Coldwell Banker, along with the stock brokerage house, Dean Witter. Its goal was to provide these services along with its many other products under one roof, thereby providing its customers with the ultimate in "one-stop shopping" convenience.

But were customers really looking for this? Did the customer really *value* the opportunity to buy a lawnmower and 100 shares of IBM at the same time and in the same place? Sears soon learned that the answer to this question was a resounding "NO!" Several years ago it admitted this failure and has reluctantly returned to its core retailing business. Its new CEO, Arthur Martinez, divested most of the service businesses and has redefined Sears' mission in the simplest terms: "Sears is a moderate-price department store."[2]

What could have gone so wrong at Sears? Professor William Torbert, professor of organizational studies at Boston College Carroll School of Management, explains this transformation to a service-oriented business was "more reactive and disjointed than proactive and coordinated."[3] According to our framework, it was not based on an instinctive or a deeply felt and informed sense of what the customer wanted and valued (external awareness) or on its core competencies (internal awareness).

Sears' foray into these services was based on what Torbert calls Type 1 thinking and control, which is predicated on the following simple but flawed formula: information gathering about the external environment, analysis of the data, a rational decision based on the various alternatives, and adjustments in the corporate structure in order to implement the final decision.[4] This neat and linear process lacks imagination; moreover, it does not tap into the corporate instinct of the organization embedded throughout the company's employees and in the countless complex relationships and alliances they have formed.

As we discussed in the early chapters, corporate instinct is a company's potent sixth sense, its intuitive ability to react in the *right* way. It is *dynamic stability* that comes about because firms with instinct manifest these four basic attributes: internal awareness, external awareness, internal responsiveness, and external responsiveness. Sears' primary problem was its lack of external awareness—its partnership with its key stakeholders was deficient and prevented the company from tuning into what the market really wanted. This led to a disturbing and costly breakdown in its external responsiveness.

Recall that one of the major traits of the instinctive organization is a decephalized decision making structure. Lamentably, Sears was cephalic—decisions were routed through the head, as in the leader at the top of the organizational pyramid, and as in an overly analytical, rational, and noninstinctive way. Sears' failure to cultivate a culture of decentralized decision making impeded its ability to transform itself successfully.

Sears also lacked internal awareness. Sears failed to capture the marvelous instinctive knowledge that resided in its human resources: its salespeople, buyers, clerks, and store managers. This knowledge is quite valuable, but it diffuses slowly throughout the organization. Sears, like so many organizations, was incapable of capturing, sharing, and creating this sort of knowledge in a useful and intelligible form. This prevented Sears from developing an active, dynamic awareness, which it needed to compete effectively in the midst of changing dynamics in the retail industry. *Sears knew that it had to transform itself, but without this instinctive awareness, it just didn't know how.*

Sears should have reinvested in its core business instead of diversifying. It should have renewed and reinvented its role as a retailer in ways that added value for its customer base. Sears is belatedly doing just that.

To avoid Sears' fate, companies must awaken the dormant instinct in the recesses of their organizations and let these instincts help shape its responsiveness. Once companies learn to exploit this resource, they will better appreciate how periodic transformations can be on target and more responsive to market needs and demands.

VIRTUES OF THE INSTINCTIVE ORGANIZATION: REASONS TO CREATE INSTINCT

The principal benefit for organizations that follow our prescription to develop corporate instinct can be summarized in two words: competitive advantage. This may manifest itself in many ways but there are at least eight benefits we believe are the most significant.

- leverage employee skills and talent
- promote a culture of decentralized decision making
- encourage social responsibility and ethical sensitivity
- develop positive stakeholder relations
- maximize return on time (ROT)
- maintain a fluid organizational structure

- create a climate of active forgetfulness and resiliency

- transcend spatial and temporal boundaries

Leverage employee skills and talent. The knowing enterprise will be able to maximize the investment in its employees; it relies on their wisdom and insight, both implicit and explicit, and lets them function collectively as leaders. This use of the full range of their knowledge and skills tends to optimize labor productivity.

Promote a culture of decentralized decision making. In this culture, employees are given the authority and knowledge to make decisions without the encumbrances of bureaucracy or hierarchy and to follow their instincts when the marketplace cannot wait. This will improve the overall quality and timeliness of decision making.

Encourage social responsibility and ethical sensitivity. Because of its keen feedback mechanisms, the instinctive enterprise is in touch with the needs and concerns of its customers. It can perceive safety or related consumer problems without obstructive "filters" or delays. This greatly improves the pace of its deliberations and the quality of its normative judgments.

Develop positive stakeholder relations. The instinctive enterprise respects the skill and autonomy of its workforce and avoids management by control and intimidation. It also seeks close collaborative and mutually beneficial relationships with suppliers and other groups by being alert and responsive to their requirements and interests.

Maximize return on time (ROT). In an innovation-based economy, the ability to utilize time efficiently is paramount. All companies must strive to "compete in time" as effectively as possible.[5] The whole structure and culture of the instinctive enterprise is geared to innovation and change, which positions it well to optimize its use of time in product development cycles *and* commercial interactions with suppliers and customers.

Further, by maximizing ROT, the instinctive enterprise will be poised to capture enviable first-mover advantages (for example, by pioneering the Internet market).

Maintain a fluid organizational structure. The knowing enterprise is not locked into one organizational format. It has the flexibility to adapt its structure to meet different market requirements and circumstances. It is the truly perpetual organization whose only fixed feature is its ability to change.

Create a climate of active forgetfulness and resiliency. The greatest power may be the power to forget the past (process memory) in order to be more creative and innovative. The instinctive enterprise avoids being dominated by burdensome traditions and outdated corporate history.[6] Without the burden of process memories and jaded routines, the corporation can enhance its spontaneous ingenuity while strengthening its powers of resiliency and flexibility in the face of marketplace fluctuations.

Transcend spatial and temporal boundaries. The knowing enterprise is especially well suited for international competition and cooperation—its empowered, independent workers and flexible organizational structure allow the cross-fertilization of ideas and technologies as these workers interact with allies and collaborators throughout the world.

This is by no means an exhaustive list, but it does represent the salient virtues and most positive characteristics of the instinctive enterprise. This list describes the corporation of the future. In a global, innovation-based, and collaborative economy, the corporation must assiduously cultivate its hidden assets—the explicit and tacit knowledge of its employees—its collective corporate instinct, or perish.

END NOTES

1. Wriston, Walter, *The Twilight of Sovereignty: How the Information Revolution Is Transforming Our World,* New York: Charles Scribner's Sons, 1992, p. 103.

2. Hitt, Michael A., et al., *Strategic Management: Competitiveness and Globalization,* Minneapolis, MN: West Publishing Company, 1996, p. 104.

3. Torbert, William, *Sources of Excellence,* Cambridge, MA: Edge/work Press, 1993, p. 57.

4. Ibid., pp. 54–55.

5. Keen, Peter G.W., *Competing in Time: Using Telecommunications for Competitive Advantage,* New York: Ballinger Publishing Company, 1988.

6. The philosopher Friedrich Nietzsche writes about a similar phenomenon in his treatise *On the Advantage and Disadvantage of History for Life,* trans. Peter Preuss (Indianapolis: Hackett Publishing Co., 1980). According to Nietzsche human beings, organizations, and cultures need a "plastic power" (plastiche Kraft), a power to forget the past and to grow out of oneself in order to create something new.

Appendix A
Evaluating Your
Corporate Instinct

It's a long step from saying to doing.

Cervantes,
Don Quixote

Athletes who run ultra-marathons know that it is essential for them to be aware of their own bodies' responses, capabilities, and limits. Success in their case depends on applying themselves according to their strengths, while working simultaneously on strengthening their weaknesses. Likewise, in an organization developing an ability to respond instinctively to change, an intuitive understanding of what can be handled, and how, is crucial.

Yet organizations seriously lack awareness of their levels of instinct. Our research shows that less than 10 percent of all companies rank themselves very high in terms of their own internal awareness (see page 251).

In this section, we look at how you can build that awareness and enhance your own corporate instinct. The Corporate IQ Test we provide here is a sampling of the sorts of questions we asked in our research and a quick indicator of how your company fares in terms of the four cells in the knowledge chain. It is based on a more extensive test we used to research this book, conducted among more than 350 organizations. Once you have taken this test, we will discuss areas you can further explore to better understand your corporate instinct.

THE CORPORATE IQ TEST

INSTRUCTIONS:

Look at the twenty-one questions below, and respond according to your overall impression of your organization. Try to be as objective as possible. Once you have answered the questions, use the scoring chart at the end to calculate your overall scores, and see how they compare to the population as a whole.

1. Does your company have an explicit initiative in place to capture and share organizational knowledge?

A. Yes.

B. No, we have decided not to implement such an initiative.

C. No, we haven't yet evaluated this.

2. What is the most important actual (as opposed to "official") method of strategic communication in your organization?

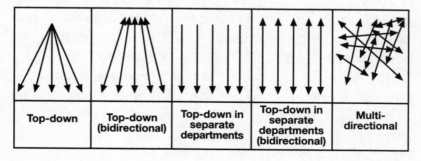

| Top-down | Top-down (bidirectional) | Top-down in separate departments | Top-down in separate departments (bidirectional) | Multi-directional |

A.   Top down

B.   Top down (bidirectional)

C.   Top down in separate departments

D.   Top down in separate departments (bidirectional)

E.   Multidirectional

3.   How prevalent in your organization is informal communication on work-related topics?

A.   Common within teams

B.   Common within business units

C.   Common across the entire organization

D.   Uncommon

4.   Which of the following statements best describes the way you would find out about knowledge in your company that may be useful to you?

A.   It is impossible to get useful knowledge about what is going on elsewhere in the company.

B.   I rely on my own personal network.

C.   I rely on several traditional approaches in the organization to finding out such knowledge, e.g., consulting the organizational chart.

D.   The company has well-organized initiatives in place to help me identify the sources of any such knowledge.

5.   Which of the following statements best describes the predominant cultural viewpoint in your organization?

A.   Each business unit minds its own business, and there is little cooperation.

B.   Cooperation between separate business units is mainly at a management level.

C. There is close cooperation at all levels between dif-
    ferent business units; however, each unit still retains
    its autonomy.

D. The whole company cooperates closely under a single
    authority structure.

6.   How realistic is the following statement of your organization? "We value an ability to learn more strongly than
a knowledge of how we currently do things."

A. Very realistic

B. Somewhat realistic

C. Average

D. Somewhat unrealistic

E. Very unrealistic

7.   How heavily does your company rely on a knowledge
of how things were done in the past?

A. Too heavily—as a result, we are ill-equipped to cope
    with current circumstances.

B. Just right—we combine the valuable lessons learned
    in the past with a fresh analysis of current circum-
    stances where required.

C. Not heavily enough—we don't sufficiently heed the
    lessons learned in the past in coping with current cir-
    cumstances.

8.   Which of the following diagrams of organizational
structure most closely resembles the way your organization actually works?

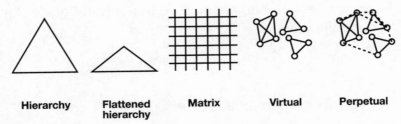

| Hierarchy | Flattened hierarchy | Matrix | Virtual | Perpetual |

A. Hierarchy

B. Flattened hierarchy

C. Matrix

D. Virtual

E. Perpetual

9. How flexible is your company's strategy, i.e., can it be adapted easily to meet the needs of changing circumstances?

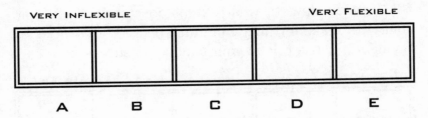

VERY INFLEXIBLE   VERY FLEXIBLE

A   B   C   D   E

10. To what extent do more junior staff members in your company participate in the design of their work?

A. They are not involved; their work is rigidly defined by more senior colleagues.

B. They have some flexibility to modify their work processes to make them more efficient.

C. They are encouraged to find new ways of doing their work.

D. They are closely involved in process redesign.

11. How often are people involved in nontraditional roles in your company?

A. Never
B. Occasionally
C. We encourage working in new roles
D. There are no traditional roles

12. How does your company prioritize time to market versus development costs in its new product initiatives?

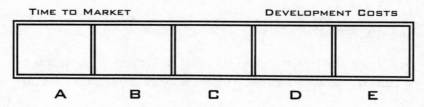

13. In your view, to what extent does serendipity (the ability to "make fortunate and unexpected discoveries by accident") play a role in your company's success?

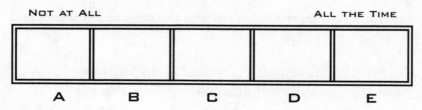

14. If a really good idea exists at the lowest ranks of your company, what is the most likely fate it will ultimately receive?

A. It will be ignored or ridiculed.
B. It will be smothered by bureaucracy.
C. It will be taken seriously and stand a good chance of implementation within your company.

D.   It will be taken seriously, but will be handled as a separate business unit or company.

E.   It will be taken outside the company by the idea's
inventors.

15.   What is your company's attitude toward skunkworks?

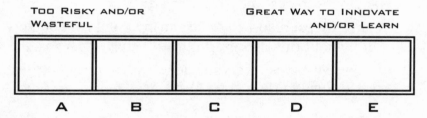

16.   How highly does your company value decentralized
decision making?

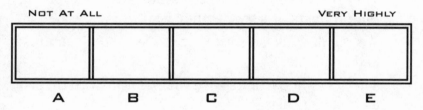

17.   Which of the following best describes the way your
company is structured?

A.   There are clear organizational boundaries and
specific points of contact with external parties.

B.   There are clear organizational boundaries, but many
close relationships with customers.

C.   We have numerous close, ongoing relationships with
outside parties—sometimes it's difficult to tell who is
in the company and who is not.

D.   The company's boundaries have largely dissolved as
partners, customer, and company employees constantly collaborate as part of a single environment.

18. What is the extent of external contact within your company?

A.   Very limited—almost no one has close contact with outside parties.

B.   Somewhat limited—management and/or some appointed groups to deal with outside parties.

C.   Fairly widespread—there are many points of contact throughout the organization with external parties.

D.   Extensive—most everyone deals with various outside parties on a fairly regular basis.

19. Which of the following statements most closely resembles your company's view of its customers?

A.   They are buyers and we are sellers—we just provide the products or services they want.

B.   We regularly liaise with them to learn their interests and concerns.

C.   They are our partners—we work closely with them on an ongoing basis.

20. Apart from customers, with which of the following external parties does your company have regular, close contact?

A.   Competitors

B.   Industry associations

C.   Partners

D.   Other associations

E.   Suppliers

21. Please indicate the predominant flow of information between your company and its customers.

WE MARKET TO THEM	BOTH	WE LISTEN TO THEM

A	B	C	D	E

22. Before checking your answers, give your company a score from 0 (nonexistent) to 5 (exceptionally high) for the attributes described in the following matrix:

	Inside Company	Outside Company
Awareness	Internal awareness Score:	Internal awareness Score: ....
Responsiveness	Internal responsiveness Score:	Internal responsiveness Score: ....

THE CORPORATE IQ TEST: ANSWERS

The Corporate IQ Test has been divided into four sets of questions, to determine a score for your company's internal awareness, internal responsiveness, external responsiveness, and external awareness. Use the scores below to allocate points to your answers.

QUESTIONS RELATED TO INTERNAL AWARENESS

1.   Any formal initiative to capture and share corporate knowledge, even if such an effort is unable to capture all

the tacit knowledge that exists in an organization, serves to enhance internal awareness. This usually takes the form of an organizational knowledgebase. Organizations that have decided against such initiatives receive points for having at least evaluated the potential need.

Scores: A=4; B=2; C=0

Your score: ....

2.   In a decentralized environment, a culture of multidirectional communication plays an important role in sharing knowledge. Communications infrastructures actually replace the functionality of hierarchical organizational structure.

Scores: A=1; B=2; C=0; D=1; E=4

Your score:...............

3.   Informal communication, rather than being wasteful, is the basis for the community of practice. It plays an important role in the exchange of "war stories," or experiences that act as learning aids in the group. Informal communication across the organization as a whole is particularly valuable, as it allows learning opportunities between people who may have very different experiences.

Scores: A=1; B=2; C=4; D=0

Your score:...............

4.   When it comes to gathering focused knowledge through the organization, some have an infrastructure that supports such an exchange. The infrastructure provides broad awareness of potential learning opportunities.

Scores: A=0; B=1; C=2; D=4

Your score:..............

5. In instinctive organizations, culture plays an important role in linking business units that no longer are connected by organizational hierarchy. This linkage increases the organization's ability to exchange knowledge and increase internal awareness.

Scores: A=0; B=2; C=4; D=2

Your score:..............

My internal awareness score (sum of scores for questions 1 to 5): ....

Divide this score by 4: ....

This is your Internal Awareness score, out of a possible total score of 5.

QUESTIONS RELATED TO INTERNAL RESPONSIVENESS

6. Probably the most basic tenet of metaskills is a commitment to learning and developing new skills. In this way, an organization is much more able to mobilize around an unexpected new opportunity very quickly and painlessly.

Scores: A=4; B=3; C=2; D=1; E=0

Your score:..............

7. An instinctive company is able to balance its leverage of valuable relevant knowledge gained from its past experiences with an openness to explore new ideas when organizational knowledge is no longer applicable to new circumstances.

Scores: A=0; B=4; C=0

Your score:..............

8.   The organizational structure is a clear manifestation of the organization's instinct. While it has relevance to all four cells of the knowledge chain, it is most pertinent to internal responsiveness, as it implies an ability to change quickly and adapt to closely match new business imperatives. Hierarchies rank low as they have little flexibility to change. Flattened hierarchies and matrix organizations show some tendencies toward instinct, while organizations able to change form and function rapidly rank highest.

Scores: A=0; B=1; C=2; D=3; E=5

Your score:..............

9.   The company's strategy itself must have the ability to address new circumstances. It should fulfill the role of a guideline to aid decision making, rather than a rigid prescription.

Scores: A=0; B=1; C=2; D=3; E=4

Your score:..............

10.   The faster and more turbulent the external business environment is, the more it is necessary for the organization to be able to reform the way in which it does work. If workers themselves are involved on a regular basis in designing their work, they will be more able to adapt it to meet specific changes in external requirements.

Scores: A=0; B=1; C=3; D=4

Your score:..............

11. An unpredictable future implies a need for flexibility of roles. Cross-skilling implies that people should at least be able to take on the roles of the people with whom they work, but instinctive organizations may even be able to deploy entire teams in new roles. This implies a high level of internal flexibility.

Scores: A=0; B=1; C=2; D=4

Your score:...............

Your internal responsiveness score (sum of scores for questions 6 to 11): ....

Divide this score by 5: ....

This is your internal responsiveness score, out of a possible total score of 5.

QUESTIONS RELATED TO EXTERNAL RESPONSIVENESS

12. The future belongs to companies that capture opportunities first. Companies seldom err on the side of time to market rather than costs. Cost savings are useless if products and processes are not implemented quickly enough to differentiate the company. Thus, an emphasis on the time it takes to respond is far more likely to pay higher dividends for the company's responsiveness—and may ensure that money is not wasted on missed opportunities.

Scores: A=4; B=3; C=2; D=1; E=0

Your score:...............

13. Serendipity is an indicator of the company's approach toward innovation. A company's "luck" is largely dependent on its levels of experimentation with new, potentially

lucrative ideas. This in turn is a factor of the decentralized structure and cultural commitment to innovation.

Scores: A=0; B=1; C=2; D=3; E=4

Your score:...............

14. A company able to accept innovation leadership from lower levels in the organization has at its disposal a portfolio of ideas, experiences, and skills that can be used as opportunities for innovation. Support of innovation at lower levels is an excellent way to nurture innovation skills and build up specific knowledge about markets and products.

Scores: A=0; B=1; C=3; D=4; E=1

Your score:...............

15. Skunkworks are a reflection of the company's commitment to learning through experimentation (including failure, if necessary), as well as its attitude toward taking risk as part of its innovation approach. Instinctive companies are able to point to many examples of wildly successful innovation initiatives which began life as "high-risk" skunkworks attempts.

Scores: A=0; B=1; C=2; D=3; E=4

Your score:..................

16. Decisions made at the point of contact with the external environment are significantly quicker than those deferred to higher corporate levels, and, in instinctive companies, these decisions are also likely to be better informed than those passed to higher levels.

Scores: A=0; B=1; C=2; D=3; E=4

Your score:..................

Your external responsiveness score (sum of scores for questions 12 to 16): ....

Divide this score by 4: ....

This is your external responsiveness score, out of a possible total score of 5.

QUESTIONS RELATED TO EXTERNAL AWARENESS

17. The broader the contact between the company and its external environment, the wider the company's experience of the external environment. People who interact regularly with outside parties do not have to rely on the organization itself to convey such knowledge to them. Also, the exposure to the diversity of the external environment is a source of stimulation for innovation.

Scores: A=0; B=2; C=3; D=4

Your score:...............

18. Instinctive organizations do not rely on appointed channels to interact with the external environment. The entire organization is opened up, and across the organization, people and teams have extensive contact with customers, partners, and even competitors.

Scores: A=0; B=1; C=3; D=4

Your score:...............

19. The traditional view of customers as buyers and companies as sellers is changing as more and more customers become intimately involved in the design and development of the products and services that are to meet their needs. This in turn stimulates the company's awareness of

the marketplace, and enables the company to meet customers' needs much more closely.

Scores: A=0; B=2; C=4

Your score:...............

20. The external environment consists not just of customers. Valuable knowledge can be gained from many industry- and non-industry-related parties. Instinctive organizations usually have close links with many, if not all, of these parties.

Scores: 0 or 1 party = 0; 2 parties = 1; 3 parties = 2; 4 parties = 3; all 5 parties = 4

Your score:...............

21. Instinctive companies have an intimate ongoing dialogue with their customers, rather than a monologue of their unique abilities. It is seldom that a company can listen too much to its customers.

Scores: A=0; B=1; C=4; D=4; E=2

Your score:...............

Your external awareness score (sum of scores for questions 17 to 21): ....

Divide this score by 4: ....

This is your external awareness score, out of a possible total score of 5.

EVALUATING YOUR CORPORATE INSTINCT

The four scores you have calculated give you an indication of your internal awareness, internal responsiveness, external responsiveness, and external awareness. Compare these scores with the four scores you estimated for your company for the same categories, in question 22. Are there any scores where your estimate differed by more than one point? These are indications of misperception of the true levels of the four characteristics in your organization.

How do you shape up in comparison to other companies? Here are the results of the Corporate IQ Test we administered:

	Very low (0-1)	Low (1-2)	Average (2-3)	High (3-4)	Very High (4-5)
Internal awareness	3%	20%	40%	28%	9%
Internal responsiveness	8%	24%	39%	25%	4%
External responsiveness	2%	18%	38%	30%	12%
External awareness	2%	17%	36%	34%	11%

Take a look at the "Very High" column—that's where your organization wants to be if it is to become instinctive. For all the world-class companies we interviewed, only around 10 percent of all organizations are in this select group. Clearly, this is because very few corporations have paid any attention to the factors of instinctiveness before. Now that you have a sense of how your company's corporate instinct shapes up, you will need to focus in on specific areas requiring attention. Take a look at the questions in each of these categories, and take note of where your organization is particularly strong or weak—these will form key leverage points for exercising your organization's instinct later.

There is no rote answer for the way in which this research should be conducted. It will be hard work, and should involve many parts of the organization. Be careful not to ignore the informal organization—the practices and structures that define how things are really done (the practical organization), as opposed to how they are supposed to be done (the prescribed organization).

Appendix B
Where To Now?

Creative thinking will improve as we relate the new fact
to the old fact and all facts to each other.

John Dewey,
American philosopher and educator

Taking the Corporate IQ test and contemplating your organization in terms of the four attributes of internal awareness, internal responsiveness, external responsiveness, and external awareness, is likely to leave you with some rough impressions of where your organization is strong or weak. But this is not enough. The factors driving the strengths and weaknesses now need to be examined.

Our research has shown that the major factors affecting external and internal awareness are corporate structure, corporate culture, strategic leadership, technology, and industry factors. In fact, if those organizations with high instinct are examined separately, the contributory factors rank as follows:

	% of respondents ranking this factor as most important					
	Corporate structure	Corporate culture	Strategic leadership	Technology	Industry factors	Other
Internal awareness	16%	31%	20%	16%	12%	6%
Internal responsiveness	16%	32%	26%	11%	11%	5%
External responsiveness	14%	21%	27%	13%	21%	6%
External awareness	10%	14%	38%	14%	14%	10%

As can be clearly seen, corporate structure, culture, and strategic leadership are the three most prominent causal factors. But what is it that drives these? During our research, we established the following list of checkpoints to monitor the evolution of corporate instinct.

- the role of knowledge
- the structure of work
- the base of skills
- the knowledge infrastructure
- attitudes toward innovation
- the organizational structure
- the corporate culture
- teams and communication
- finding pockets of instinct

These should be used to guide further investigations into your company. Using each checkpoint one at a time, try to think of concrete cases where your company exhibits strong tendencies, either toward or away from instinct.

THE ROLE OF KNOWLEDGE

Think about the industry in which your company currently operates. Is it primarily production oriented, where getting the job done cheaply and quickly is the number one priority? Or is this insufficient to ensure your company's competitiveness? Technological progress around the world has eroded companies' abilities in their industries to distinguish themselves based on price, quality, or features—these are now regarded as standard requirements for competing in most industries. In the face of looming competitive threats, market leaders are realizing that the only way to stay ahead is to keep working to be the best. It should be no surprise that our research indicated that 80 percent of all companies rank innovation as the primary competitive factor—in even the most staid industries, from banking to retailing to farming. Those companies focusing on innovation as the most important competitive criterion consistently have higher corporate instinct—and are 56 percent more likely to be responsive in their external environments than the world at large. What is the knowledge content of your company's products and processes—how much of the value of the products and processes is due to knowledge that your organization uniquely possesses? What percentage of the people in your company could be described as knowledge workers? Corporate instinct is typically far more developed among those companies working in knowledge industries—and the true knowledge companies, those where all workers can be described as knowledge workers, are 75 percent more likely to have high external responsiveness levels. If knowledge is a dominant force in your industry, it is quite possible that your company has a fairly strong instinct in action already. Conversely, if you work in a mature industry with little innovation, your corporate instinct will much more likely be dormant, and will have to be awakened. We found that companies in mature industries are 40 percent less likely to have high levels of corporate instinct.

THE STRUCTURE OF WORK

Think about the work you and others perform in your organization. Do people in your company have a formal job description? How frequently does what they actually do differ from what their job description prescribes? Most likely, if your company is in a mature industry, many of the processes and roles are well defined and clearly laid out. These processes do not change frequently and are often quite suited to a mechanistic approach. Innovation, on the other hand, is not so clear-cut. Many processes involving innovation cannot be defined clearly, and may in fact change form as they occur. They rely heavily on people's knowledge and intelligence to fill in the gaps—gaps that cannot be plugged entirely by technology. Here, work is far more unstructured, and broad guidelines are more common than strict rules. The responses to the Corporate IQ Test reveal that highly responsive and innovative companies provide broad goals defining job descriptions, but allow for circumstances to shape the detail—often through a process managed by the workers themselves.

How is work designed in your company? Are your corporate processes the result of regimented management-driven time-and-motion reengineering studies, or do they evolve in response to changing circumstances? Companies involving employees in shaping their work have much greater flexibility to adapt to changing circumstances, and as a result, they are five times more likely to rank highly for responsiveness, according to the Corporate IQ Test.

THE BASE OF SKILLS

Corporate instinct assumes a certain level of expertise throughout the organization. More than mere skills, it demands an ability to achieve results. If people are to take responsibility for responsive decision making upon themselves, management needs to be assured that they are well equipped to perform the role. How quickly are people expected to adapt their skill sets to meet new challenges? Are people frequently challenged to work outside of their nominal skills areas? Instinctive organizations work hard to ensure that all members of the organization have the ability not only to perform their work, but to reinvent the work—either by making it more efficient, or by opening up additional avenues for business, or both. Instinctive organizations are three times more likely than average organizations to prefer a well-honed learning ability in their employees rather than an experience of how things are usually done. Also, instinctive organizations are twice as likely to generate innovations from nontraditional sources throughout the organization, including nonmanagement individuals and teams that are not explicitly charged with this task.

THE KNOWLEDGE INFRASTRUCTURE

While most organizations today rely heavily upon innovation for competitive advantage, many are beginning only now to put into place an infrastructure to ensure the integrity and usefulness of their organizational knowledge. Our research shows that less than half of all organizations have an explicit initiative under way to capture organizational knowledge and make it widely available. How are the business activities in your organization captured? What proportion is captured in the products themselves, in process and product documentation, and in the minds of people themselves? Our research shows that in four out of ten companies, the primary repository for corporate knowledge is employees' minds—which go home with them at the end of each day, and go to your competitor when they quit.

Do people become indispensable to the way things are done in your company? How heavily does your company rely on individuals' personal experience? Great emphasis should also be placed on ensuring that skills can be captured in more than one person, and that each person is able to adapt their existing skill sets or develop new ones as the need arises. For corporate instinct to be effective, knowledge must be captured in the organization as a whole, rather than merely implicitly in a few scattered brain trusts. In this way, the organization avoids exposing itself to damaging losses of key people who are the only repositories of the organization's valuable knowledge resources. Companies that have separated corporate know-how from the ethereal realms of experts' heads and captured them as far as possible in technological or team-based alternative repositories are able to make this information more widely available throughout the organization, thereby increasing their ability to respond more flexibly and quickly to external influences. Informal internal networks of workers who share such knowledge are a common approach, and should be encouraged.

ATTITUDES TOWARD INNOVATION

How does your organization feel about change? Is it enthusiastic, accepting, or afraid? Is change generally regarded as an opportunity or a threat? The more a company is able to complement change rather than attempting to constrain it, the better its corporate instinct. Capturing corporate knowledge is of little use if it is not used properly. The most effective use of captured knowledge is spreading it as widely as possible throughout the organization, and then leveraging it to construct innovative solutions to problems. The organization's approach toward innovation is a major determinant of corporate instinct—a risk-friendly approach by management toward experimentation and idea creation, irrespective of the consequences, is likely to be reciprocated by the spontaneous generation of skunkworks attempts across the organization. On the other hand, if innovation efforts are channeled through specific business areas and according to rigid guidelines, then much of the organization's ability to respond is lost. Our research has shown that companies generally rate themselves highly for intelligence, innovation, and vision, and give exceptionally high rankings for innovation as a competitive factor in their industries. Yet almost two-thirds of them make little or no use of skunkworks as a means for driving innovation. More than half of them admit that failed skunkworks attempts have scared them off this form of innovation. This does not mean that all their skunkworks efforts have proved to be bad business, rather that they are afraid to continue with what they see as risky investments. These same companies acknowledge that serendipity (the ability to "make unfortunate and unexpected discoveries by accident") plays only a minor role in their ability to innovate. For those that do make these accidental discoveries, they would attest that luck has nothing to do with their success. On the contrary, statistics show that these risk-friendly companies have levels of external awareness and responsiveness that are as much as one-third higher than more risk-averse companies.

THE ORGANIZATIONAL STRUCTURE

Is your company control oriented or collaboration oriented? In other words, to what extent are power brokers prepared to relinquish power for the good of the company? The less the dominant influence of management on the corporation, the greater the likelihood that the company is exercising its corporate instinct. If there is a sense of parity among different parts of the organization about their ability to contribute to the company, teamwork is likely to be greater and instinct as well. Our research results revealed that people feel they are highly regarded as key assets in their organizations, yet almost half say the predominant organizational structure which most closely resembles the way their organization actually works is a hierarchy or flattened hierarchy, where control is not yet diffused to other organizational experts.

THE CORPORATE CULTURE

Most of the organizations we have surveyed believe that corporate culture plays a disproportionately high role in shaping their instinct, especially their internal awareness and responsiveness. This is not surprising—people's emotional and psychological responses are shaped by the dominant emotions in the organization. What is the real culture in your company—not the one management embraces in its mission and vision, unless that is the same as the grassroots way of thinking and feeling? Who sets the cultural tone in your organization? Is it managerial prescription or grass-roots evolution? Our research has shown that the most important cultural messages in instinctive organizations are organization-wide commitment to autonomy and empowerment, since they free employees to take on the roles of decision makers. Try to examine to what extent people are encouraged to take ownership of the processes and products in which they are directly involved, and to what extent that ownership is interfered with by management.

TEAMS AND COMMUNICATION

What is the turnover of teams in your company? If your teams are institutionalized, it's probably because it's so difficult to construct the team in the first place, and holding the team together once they are constructed becomes the most economical approach. But this approach restricts the people who can become members of teams, and the flexibility they have to draw in new people or change their points of view. Instinctive organizations often have teams that are spontaneously created, draw upon any resources, wherever they may be, according to the specific conditions they find themselves in, and evaporate as quickly. In our research we found that some teams last for as little as a week, before dissolving and recombining in a different form.

Examine how teams in your company are structured—do they parallel organizational structure, or are they drawn from across the organization, depending on team members' merits and the specific needs of the project? Instinctive companies are almost twice as likely to be made up of teams from across the organization, according to members' specific skills and the needs of the project.

Also take a look at the barriers to communication that may exist. How easy is it to reach people, irrespective of where they are geographically, hierarchically, and in time? It is imperative that an organization that strives to have corporate instinct develops a powerful, seamless communication infrastructure, both within the organization and outside it.

FINDING POCKETS OF INSTINCT

It's unlikely you'll find corporate instinct evenly distributed throughout your organization, especially if it has arisen spontaneously. Different management approaches and personalities throughout the organization have encouraged or suppressed it. Many companies can testify to the fact that fantastic innovations or new approaches started "out there" in some extreme part of the organization, usually one much closer to the marketplace. These areas of unharnessed instinct usually occur in the noisiest part of the company, where there is the most creative activity, even the most disruption. Look for the irregularities, the things that don't fit in to the structure of everyday corporate life. Talk to the road warriors, the customer representatives, the people in remote branch offices—anyone who doesn't live in the same corporate environment as the management team. Don't expect to find these areas in the same place on every organizational chart. They are most visible underground, and identifying them requires using the informal networks of communication in the company. Put an ear to the ground in your organization: what war stories are going around? Monitor the bulletin boards, the water cooler, the mailing lists. Think of our example of John Gage at Sun Microsystems, who does not rely on his company's organizational chart to determine the real priorities and spheres of influence in Sun. He looks at the names on the electronic mailing lists that he subscribes to in order to determine the people that count.

Why do so few organizations have high instinct today? Simply because so few of them have realized that they need it. You have taken the first step in developing your corporation's instinct by taking the Corporate IQ Test. It gives you a reliable indication of where you can get started in developing your organization's corporate instinct. We have found that just making organizations aware of where they are weak and strong is a significant enabling step in their development of corporate instinct.

Your corporate instinct is waiting to be awakened. Find out where it is, and find out where it can be strengthened. You will be embarking on a path few other companies have—a path that will lead you to the future first.

Appendix C
The Language of
Corporate Instinct

We have introduced many new terms and concepts in this book and so we have provided a glossary to help readers understand the new language of corporate instinct. Most of these definitions are concise but are elaborated upon in the book. We also include other terms that have not originated in this book but may still be unfamiliar to some of our readers.

adaptive learning: identifying a gap between where one is and where one needs to be and taking the necessary measures to close the gap

cephalic: the approach to decision making found in command-and-control organizations that route decisions through a central brain or "head"

community of practice: communities that form within an organization where people assume roles based on their abilities and skills instead of titles and hierarchical stature

continuous reengineering: people who know the most about a process are the ones who work on it and *redesign it on an ongoing basis as needed*

corporate amnesia: loss of collective experience, embedded tacit knowledge, and accumulated skills usually through excessive downsizings and layoffs

corporate instinct: corporate instinct is a company's collective sixth sense regarding its ability to overcome its own memory and respond instantaneously and effectively to market opportunity, customers, and competition

corporate memory: corporations, like individuals, remember the past, including long-standing processes and procedures along with corporate traditions and values; memory is strategically important, but sometimes it can be a serious liability if it inhibits an organization from adjusting quickly to its changing environment

decephalization: represents a corporation's ability to sense the market with its extremities and not just its head, that is, companies rely on all their employees to sense the need for change and to collaborate in key decisions

disintermediation: elimination of middle layers of management control and other internal or external intermediaries; the benefit is a faster knowledge chain

enterprise-wide information systems: a tool of corporate instinct—they provide a comprehensive overview of the business and the industry in which it competes; an example of such a system might be a comprehensive data warehouse

federation: perpetual enterprises will be loosely organized as an alliance of workcells in place of departments or divisions

generative learning: sometimes needed to accompany adaptive learning when the gap between where one is and where one aspires to be requires new ways of perceiving or thinking

instinct: the spontaneous application of acquired and latent intelligence to unknown situations within an unspecified context

intellectual capital: the intangible assets of information and knowledge which are quite different from other forms of capital

knowing enterprise: the enlightened organization with instinct and accompanying self-awareness; this enterprise has intimate, constantly renewed knowledge about itself, its capabilities, resources, and opportunities

knowledge chain: corporate instinct, the dynamic adaptability of companies, stems from the four definitive stages in this chain: internal awareness, internal responsiveness, external responsiveness, and external awareness

knowledge management: process of capturing organizational knowledge and expertise and representing it electronically

matrix organization: synthesis of central control and decentralization structures within a single organization

metaskills: the basic tool of generative learning; these skills are aimed at ensuring three things: skills adaptability, autonomous decision making, and an emotional aptitude for change

perpetual organization: an organization that is without any permanent structure; it takes on whatever form is suitable for current conditions and market demands

process asset: anything unique to the way an organization runs its business, including activities as diverse as training, marketing, manufacturing, etc.

return on time (ROT): metric for how well the knowledge chain is working; since instinct reduces the time required to go through this cycle, it increases a company's velocity and return on time

tacit knowledge: experiential know-how based on clues, hunches, instinct, and personal insights; distinct from formal, explicit knowledge

virtual organization: companies "without walls" and without many permanent employees; it relies on contractual relationships with suppliers, distributors, and a contingent workforce

workcell: a collection of roles within an organization; individuals in these cells are distinguished by their flexibility and adaptability

workflow: one of the tools of corporate instinct—a set of computer-based methodologies that enable the analysis, compression, and automation of business activities

Appendix D
Recommended
Readings

Below is a list of books and articles that have stimulated our reflections about corporate instinct and many of the other related topics discussed in this book.

BOOKS

Barabba, Vincent P., *Meeting of the Minds: Creating the Market-Based Enterprise,* Boston: Harvard Business School Press, 1995.

Bennis, Warren, *Changing Organizations,* New York: McGraw-Hill, 1966.

Brooking, Annie, *Intellectual Capital Core Asset for the Third Millennium Enterprise,* Boston: International Thompson Business Press, 1996.

Champy, James, and Michael Hammer, *Reengineering the Corporation,* New York: Harper Business Books, 1993.

Davenport, Thomas, *Process Innovation: Reengineering Work Through Information Technology*, Boston: Harvard Business School Press, 1993.

Davidow, William, and Michael Malone, *The Virtual Corporation*, New York: HarperBusiness, 1992.

De Geus, Arie, *The Living Company*, Boston: Harvard Business School Press, 1997.

Drucker, Peter, *Managing for the Future: The 1990s and Beyond*, New York: Truman Valley Books/Dutton, 1992.

Edvinsson, Leif, and Malone, Michael S., *Intellectual Capital: Realizing Your Company's True Value by Finding Its Hidden Brainpower*, New York: Harper-Business, Division of HarperCollins Publishers, 1997.

Hamermesh, Richard G., *Fad-Free Management: The Six Principles That Drive Successful Companies and Their Leaders*, Santa Monica: Knowledge Exchange, LLC, 1996.

Helgesen, Sally, *The Web of Inclusion*, New York: Currency Doubleday, 1995.

Keen, Peter G.W., *Competing in Time: Using Telecommunications for Competitive Advantage*, New York: Ballinger Publishing Company, 1988.

Leonard-Barton, Dorothy, *Wellsprings of Knowledge*, Boston: Harvard Business School Press, 1995.

Lipnack, Jessica, and Stamps, Jeffrey, *The Age of the Network*, New York: John Wiley and Sons, Inc., 1994.

Mankin, Don, *Teams and Technology: Fulfilling the Promise of the New Organization,* Boston: Harvard Business School Press, 1996.

Marshall, Edward, *Transforming the Way We Work: The Power of the Collaborative Workplace,* New York: AMACOM, 1995.

McGill, Michael, and Slocum, John, *The Smarter Organization: How to Build a Business that Learns and Adapts to Marketplace Needs,* New York: John Wiley & Sons, Inc., 1994.

McKenney, James, *Waves of Change,* Boston: Harvard Business School Press, 1995.

Morgan, Gareth, *Images of Organization,* London: Sage Publications, 1997.

Nonaka, Ikujiro, and Takeuchi, Hirotaka, *The Knowledge-Creating Company: How Japanese Companies Create the Dynamics of Innovation,* New York: Oxford University Press, 1996.

Perkins, D.N., *Knowledge as Design,* Hillsdale, NJ: Lawrence Erlbaum Associates, Publishers, 1986.

Polanyi, Michael, *Knowing and Being,* edited by Marjorie Greene, Chicago: University of Chicago Press, 1969.

Polanyi, Michael, *Personal Knowledge: Toward a Post-Critical Philosophy,* New York: Harper Torchbooks, 1962.

Quinn, James Brian, *Intelligent Enterprise: A Knowledge and Service-Based Paradigm for Industry,* New York: The Free Press, 1992.

Selznick, Philip, *Leadership in Administration,* Evanston, IL: Row Peterson and Company, 1957.

Senge, Peter, *The Fifth Discipline,* New York: Currency Doubleday, 1990.

Sloan, Alfred, *My Years with General Motors,* New York: Doubleday, 1964.

Stewart, Thomas A., *Intellectual Capital: The New Wealth of Organizations,* New York: Currency Doubleday, 1997.

Torbert, William, *Sources of Excellence,* Cambridge, MA: Edge/Work Press, 1993.

Wriston, Walter, *The Twilight of Sovereignty: How the Information Revolution Is Transforming Our World,* New York: Charles Scribner's Sons, 1992.

Zuboff, Shosanna, *In the Age of the Smart Machine,* New York: Basic Books, 1989.

ARTICLES

Arthur, W. Brian, "Increasing Returns and the New World of Business," *Harvard Business Review,* July/August 1996.

Chesbrough, Henry, and Tecce, David, "When is Virtual Virtuous? Organizing for Innovation," *Harvard Business Review,* January/February 1996.

Davenport, Thomas H., "Saving IT's Soul: Human-Centered Information Management," *Harvard Business Review,* March/April 1994.

Davis, Stan, and Botkin, Jim, "The Coming of Knowledge-Based Business," *Harvard Business Review*, September/October 1994.

De Geus, Arie, "The Living Company," *Harvard Business Review*, March/April 1997.

Drucker, Peter, "The Age of Social Transformation, Part III," *Quality Digest*, April 1995.

Drucker, Peter, "The Coming of the New Organization," *Harvard Business Review*, January/February 1988.

Kelly, Kevin, "The Economics of Ideas," *Wired*, June 1996.

Lipton, Mark, "Demystifying the Development of an Organizational Vision," *Sloan Management Review*, Summer 1996.

Mintzberg, Henry, "Crafting Strategy," *Harvard Business Review*, July/August 1987.

Nonaka, Ikujiro, "The Knowledge-Creating Company," *Harvard Business Review*, November/December 1991

Quinn, James Brian, Anderson, Philip, and Finkelstein, Sydney, "Managing Professional Intellect: Making the Most of the Best," *Harvard Business Review*, March/April 1996.

Uhlfelder, Helene, "Why Teams Don't Work," *Quality Digest*, June 1994.

Zuboff, Shoshana, "Informate the Enterprise: An Agenda for the Twenty-First Century," in Case et al., *Building the Information Age Organization*, Burr Ridge, IL: IRWIN, 1994.

Index